Dog In My Footsteps

Dog In My Footsteps

More stories of a vet's wife

CHRYSTAL SHARP

Illustrations by Jason Bronkhorst

27. 12. 2002.

Dear Stams,
   Much Love
      Chrystal.

PENGUIN BOOKS

PENGUIN BOOKS

Published by the Penguin Group
80 Strand, London WC2R 0RL, England
Penguin Putnam Inc, 375 Hudson Street, New York,
New York 10014, USA
Penguin Books Australia Ltd, 250 Camberwell Road, Camberwell,
Victoria 3124, Australia
Penguin Books Canada Ltd, 10 Alcorn Avenue, Toronto, Ontario,
Canada M4V 3B2
Penguin Books (NZ) Ltd, Cnr Rosedale and Airborne Roads, Albany,
Auckland, New Zealand
Penguin Books India (P) Ltd, 11 Community Centre, Panchsheel Park,
New Delhi – 110 017, India
Penguin Books (South Africa) (Pty) Ltd, 24 Sturdee Avenue, Rosebank,
Johannesburg 2196, South Africa

Penguin Books (South Africa) (Pty) Ltd, Registered Offices:
Second Floor, 90 Rivonia Road, Sandton 2196, South Africa

First published by Penguin Books (South Africa) (Pty) Ltd 2002

Copyright © Text Chrystal Sharp 2002
Copyright © Illustrations Jason Bronkhorst
All rights reserved
The moral right of the author has been asserted

ISBN 0143 02414 0

Typeset by CJH Design in 10.5 on 13.5 Palatino
Cover Design: Mouse Design
Printed and bound by Interpak Books, KwaZulu-Natal

Except in the United States of America, this book is sold subject
to the condition that it shall not, by way of trade or otherwise,
be lent, resold, hired out or otherwise circulated without the
publisher's prior consent in any form of binding or cover other
than that in which it is published and without a similar condition
including this condition being imposed on the subsequent purchaser.

To absent friends . . .

Contents

Foreword ix
Basic Instincts 1
The Nature of Things 22
Splitting Up 43
On Foreign Shores 54
Moving On 63
The Doppelgänger 73
At a Push 84
Changing Pace 97
To the Heart of the Matter 107
Subterranean Rumblings 120
Dyed in the Wool 134
A Whiff of Revolt 146
Parrot Fashion 156
Filling the Gaps 166
At the Drop of a Hat 176
Hidden Treasures 184
Laying it on thick 193
Spirit Levels 203
Smash and Grab 214
Sealed with a Fish 225
Dogging My Footsteps 238

They stroll into your life
Leaving footprints everywhere

On the floors
On the tables
Even on the walls

But the footprints
You cannot wipe away
Are those that they leave

Across your heart

Foreword

Like a breath of fresh air, the long-awaited sequel to *If The Cat Fits* has breezed into our lives. Picking up where *Cat* left off, Chrystal Sharp's new book chronicles the next five years in the life and times of a vet in a small coastal town in the Eastern Cape as seen through the eyes of his effervescent wife.

Sometimes wacky, often moving, but always engaging, *Dog In My Footsteps* is a lively account of the family's assimilation into their new community. Chrystal's grudging tolerance of the follies and foibles of the human race, combined with offerings from the many animals who share her life, give us a narrative that is both hilarious and thought-provoking.

Those who enjoyed her first book will not be disappointed for all the elements that made it such a delight are back in abundance. This new window into Chrystal's world has one succumbing to the notion that one is visiting an old family friend.

Chrystal's stories are a celebration of all that is simple and beautiful in life – a welcome tonic in the stressful times in which we live. And, whilst being entertained, we are subliminally compelled to examine our role as custodians of the planet, and all that this requires of us. Herein lies the substance that makes this charming book more than just the fun read that it appears to be.

Once again, it is a fitting tribute to Chrystal and her family's commitment to promoting 'the health and welfare of animals and mankind' that this book, like its predecessor, will be instrumental in helping vets create a system of delivery – through the Community Veterinary Clinics initiative – that seeks to give all South African animal caregivers access to essential veterinary services.

Dean Sim BVSc
Chairman, Animal Welfare & Community Development Committee of SAVA
Co-ordinator, National Community Veterinary Clinics Initiative of SAVA

Basic Instincts

Daylight was seeping into the sky and the rich pungent smell of the sea wafted in through the open bedroom windows. Ensconced in the duvet I lay back in bed, dreamily contemplating the day.

Suddenly I heard a sound coming from the sitting room. A tick-tack on the linoleum. 'Tick-tack . . . tick-tack.' I tensed, trying to identify the sound. It couldn't be the dogs, I thought, they were still fast asleep.

'Tick-tack . . . tick-tack flip.'

There was a stealthiness to it, as if someone was pausing to see if we had heard. Wide awake now, and slightly alarmed, I wondered if we were being burgled.

'Tick-tack flip . . . tick-tack tick-tack flip.'

The sound approached our open bedroom door and then ceased abruptly.

'Dave,' I whispered, nudging his gently snoring form. He grunted once and turned over.

'Dave, wake-up . . . there's someone in the house.'

'Wha?'

'There's someone walking around in the house,' I muttered urgently. As he opened his eyes, I placed a finger over my lips. We stared at each other for a second and then, as one, we sat up in bed.

A penguin was standing on the carpeted floor at the foot of the bed, staring up at us hopefully.

'Parker!' we exclaimed.

A couple of months earlier I had been assisting Dave in the surgery when a young man named Nigel Parker arrived with a penguin in his arms.

'At least, I think it's a penguin,' I murmured doubtfully.

We had been living at the coast for several months, and by this time I was able to differentiate between an adult and a baby penguin. But this one resembled neither. Clumps of feathers were clustered on top of its head, giving it the look of a mad professor. One who, in the heat of his experiments, had forgotten to comb his hair. The rest of its body appeared equally bizarre. Smooth sleek patches of feathers alternated with loose untidy tufts.

'What's wrong with its feathers?' I asked Dave.

'I'm not sure. It looks as if it's moulting.'

He placed the penguin in a shallow cardboard box while I fetched a pilchard from the freezer. I thawed the fish in warm water and cut it into small slivers. While I held the penguin upright, Dave opened its beak and placed a sliver in its mouth. It swallowed the first sliver and Dave slowly fed it the rest.

'It's terribly thin,' I observed. 'Underneath the feathers it's skin and bone.'

The slivers of fish seemed to kindle a spark of interest in its eyes. All is not lost, that look seemed to say. While there's fish, there's hope.

Over the next few days the penguin gradually gained

strength and began swallowing whole fish. When it moved, puffs of tiny feathers would float from its body forming a downy carpet at its feet. After a week it had shed most of the loose feathers and from underneath them the plumage of an adult emerged. Dave phoned a zoologist at one of the universities and learned that penguins moult once a year. From start to finish the moult takes approximately three weeks and during this time, because of lack of insulation, they cannot hunt effectively in the sea.

'They usually feed themselves up prior to a moult,' the zoologist explained, 'but problems arise when they enter a moult without sufficient physical reserves.'

We realised that Parker must have entered his moult physically unprepared. After two weeks at the surgery he began to put on weight and we decided to move him to the house.

'He can decide for himself when he is ready to go back to sea,' Dave said.

And so Parker became one of the family. During the day he would drift around the front garden or simply relax in the sun. At night we would close him in the patio area off the kitchen for his own safety, knowing that there were wild cats in the surrounding bush.

As far as the tame cats were concerned, one of them was not terribly thrilled by Parker's arrival.

'What the HELL is that?' Splittie hissed explosively, shielding Seafood with her body.

'It's a penguin, you've seen one before.'

'Not loose in the front garden. Can't you lock it up somewhere? I won't have Seafood exposed to this kind of thing.'

'It's deciding when to go to sea again.'

'Well,' she glared, *'let's hope it arrives at a decision soon.'*

I sighed. Predictably, Splittie had added penguins to her

list of dislikes. Penguins and all other marine life, I thought cynically.

Dave and I had adopted Splittie, a crippled grey-and-white tabby, shortly after we were married. Dave had been doing a locum in a veterinary practice on the Natal south coast when she was brought in, in a closed cardboard box, crippled, pregnant and semi-wild.

For Splittie, apart from her fur, there were no grey areas. Life was black or white. She either liked something or she didn't. Her list of dislikes was long and detailed. It included our greyhound Whippy, all other dogs, Italian epileptic cats, all other foreigners, baby monkeys, all other wildlife, goats, all other livestock, and strangers. Her list of likes was short and final: her daughter Seafood, me, Dave and our son Nic.

Much to Splittie's disgust, in the days that followed Parker showed no inclination to go off to sea. He pottered around the garden taking a keen interest in our activities. If I was gardening, he would peer into the hole I had just dug, or rifle through the pile of weeds at my feet. Nic's toys, scattered around the lawn, were a source of constant fascination. Totally absorbed, he'd investigate objects with his beak, nudging them around the lawn to see how they worked. It occurred to me that penguins might be very inquisitive.

Then one morning when Nic, the dogs and cats and I set off down the path to the beach, he tagged along behind. While Nic splashed in the shallows with his bucket and spade, Parker found a rock pool nearby. I watched in fascination as he frolicked and dived, disappearing from sight only to surface again suddenly like a cork from a champagne bottle. As he swam, he swivelled on to one side and then on to the other, movements of joyful exuberance. After about thirty minutes he clambered out on to a rock, shook himself briskly and began preening his feathers, running his beak over the oil gland just above his tail several times. When he was finally satisfied with the state of his plumage he stood and basked in the sun. Like an ancient sun-worshipper. Watching him, I wondered if today was the day?

I needn't have wondered. When I stood up and took Nic by the hand and began walking slowly towards the path, Parker hopped off his rock and hurried after us. Not today, Josephine!

At the foot of the path I paused, waiting for him to catch up. As I stood there gazing out to sea, a woman who had been collecting shells approached. She looked slightly bemused.

'Is this your pigeon?' she asked, pointing at Parker.

I stared at her expressionlessly and then I looked down at Parker. He gazed back up at me. 'Yes,' I nodded. 'Yes, I think so.'

Weeks passed and, despite his daily swims, Parker showed no desire to go off into the big blue yonder.

'Isn't it about time you went off to find your roots?' I heard Splittie say to him sternly one morning. *'Do you not have family of your own?'*

Her words must have struck some chord because late that afternoon when I went to look for him, he was nowhere to be found. I searched the garden, but to no avail. Finally, I walked down the path on to the beach and there in the sand a clear trail of penguin prints headed straight into the water. Feeling somehow bereft, I wandered back up to the house.

'I hope you're satisfied now,' I said to Splittie.

She shot me a smug look, not bothering to comment.

'I hope he's going to be all right,' I said to Dave that evening.

'I'm sure he'll be fine.'

As the days went by, I scanned the beach and sea anxiously, hoping to see some sign of Parker. After two weeks had passed I accepted the fact that he had returned to his natural environment.

And now this! He was back after three weeks at sea! Amazingly, he had managed to find his way back to the right beach and the right path and the right house. Even the right bedroom!

'Who's a clever bird then?' I cooed, thrilled to see him. He seemed equally delighted and followed me through to the kitchen, where I took a few fish out to thaw. He was a bit on the thin side but nowhere near his original emaciated state.

Parker remained with us for three days, consuming breakfast, lunch and supper from a menu that didn't vary. Pilchards, pilchards and more pilchards. Wanting him to be free to come and go as he pleased, we decided not to close him in at night.

On the morning of the fourth day we woke to find him gone – this time permanently. Once again, my joy at his return to the sea was tinged with sadness but at least we knew now that he could cope.

We were happy that Parker had been able to decide for himself when he was ready to go back to sea. The fact that the house we were renting was right on the seafront made this possible.

Dave and I had been married for almost three years when

we moved to Dolphin Bay, a small town on the Eastern Cape coast, where Dave opened his own veterinary practice. Prior to this, he had done locums all over South Africa and had then accepted a post in Swaziland.

We loved Swaziland but a few months after we moved there I fell pregnant, and six months into the pregnancy I'd undergone a splenectomy at Johannesburg General Hospital, because of a very low blood platelet count. Despite a barrage of tests, the cause of the platelet problem could not be determined and in the end we had no choice but to leave Swaziland and relocate to Johannesburg in order to be near the medical facilities there.

Dave found employment as an assistant in a multi-man veterinary practice in Johannesburg, and two weeks after we arrived our son Nic was born by emergency Caesarean. When Nic was eight and a half months old we moved to Dolphin Bay.

I had never really adapted to the claustrophobic lifestyle of a big city and when we moved to the coast I thanked God every day for the exquisite natural beauty of our surroundings. To be able to wake up to the sound of waves breaking on the shore and to smell the sea air and feel the mist on my skin was a privilege I knew I'd never take for granted. Nic loved living near the sea and the animals loved it too.

The cats exulted in the freedom of being able to explore the bushy dunes and even get their feet wet in the shallows if they chose, although it took some of them a while to understand how the sea actually worked.

On one of his early forays to the beach Nuggie, our short-haired ginger cat, made the mistake of stretching out along the waterline – with his back to the sea. Fortunately the wave which swept over him was only a little one.

'Where did THAT come from?' he spluttered indignantly, a

strand of seaweed draped over his head.

'That's what waves do. They come in and they go out.'

'Are you sure?'

'Yes.'

Nuggie had come from a disadvantaged background. As a young kitten, he had been attacked by red ants and shortly after this he'd almost succumbed to pneumonia. The pneumonia had left him with chronic sinus problems and a poor self-image. The fact that Splittie often exhorted him to *'Wipe that bloody nose, will you?'* didn't help matters. But when we moved to the coast, I noticed a subtle change in him. The scenic beauty seemed to strike a creative chord in him and before long he developed a keen interest in poetry. Both reading and composing.

He'd stand gazing up at a sunset, transfixed.

'How would you describe that sky?' he'd ask. *'Is it red?'*

'More of a muted crimson, I think.'

'It's the colour of a mouse's guts,' Philby offered helpfully.

'PHILBY, that's disgusting!'

'I was only pointing out . . .'

'Well don't! What should he write . . . Shall I compare thee to a mouse's guts?'

'Well, it's easier to find a word that rhymes with "guts" than one that rhymes with "crimson".'

'That's not the point. Anyway it doesn't have to rhyme.'

'But I thought . . .'

'Never mind what you thought.'

Philby was a long-haired, mottled grey tabby, with a white bib and white feet and a beautiful plume of a tail. He and his brother Carrots, also long-haired but ginger, had been brought in for euthanasia by owners who no longer wanted them while Dave was doing a locum in the Western Cape. Initially we had taken them in with the idea of finding homes for them.

Two weeks was all it took for them to insert themselves firmly into our lives.

Philby had Machiavellian tendencies and when he wasn't pushing everyone's buttons, or daydreaming about the valley of a thousand budgies, he spent his days tracking leopard in the dunes. Ever since our stay in Swaziland he'd had a thing about leopards and snakes. Fortunately the area we were living in appeared devoid of snakes, but we had heard of two leopards living in the dune fields.

One morning, with Carrots listening wide-eyed, I heard him describing a leopard to Silverkitty, a large silver and black striped tomcat who had arrived on our doorstep soon after we moved into the house on the seafront. He wasn't very forthcoming about his past and all I had managed to establish was that a reformatory was involved.

'They're big and yellow and they have spots,' Philby explained knowledgeably.

'What colour are their spots?'

'Black.'

'Ah,' Silverkitty nodded. *'And how big are leopards exactly?'*

'Much bigger than us,' said Carrots, glancing over his shoulder nervously. He didn't really share Philby's interest in wildlife and often found himself dragged into dangerous situations unwittingly.

'Quite frankly, when it comes to a challenge I've always preferred seagulls myself,' Silverkitty remarked and the three of them paused to gaze speculatively at the seagulls clattering overhead.

'What would you like for lunch today?' I interrupted hastily, an image of Philby with a seagull slung over his shoulder flashing into my mind.

'Anything except fish,' announced Splittie, stomping up to

join the group. Her stunted body and crippled hindlegs may have been infirm but her views certainly weren't. And now she had taken against fish.

'What's wrong with fish?' I asked. 'We're living at the coast now, you know, and "When in Rome . . ."'

'I VERY much doubt that the Romans ate fish EVERY day,' she sneered, wrinkling her nose as if it had been assailed by a nasty odour.

'But I don't . . .'

'Anyway,' she added dismissively, *'Seafood doesn't like fish.'* As if that was the end of that.

'Well, that's a bit ironic,' I said, 'considering her name.'

'I was not the one who gave her the name,' she observed cuttingly.

'OK then, what about tinned beef?'

Seafood's every movement had been closely monitored by her mother from the moment she was born. Even to the extent that, although Splittie hated getting sea sand between her toes, she would stomp down on to the beach, grimly determined to keep a watchful eye on Seafood at all times. She's most probably ordered her not to like fish, I thought as I spooned the beef into seven saucers and then went to wake Fluffy who was asleep on the couch.

Fluffy was a thirteen-year-old, mink-coloured Persian cross who we had adopted just before we left Johannesburg. Her elderly owner had passed away and her two sons had brought her in to Dave for euthanasia because they didn't want her.

'Lunch is ready,' I bellowed into her ear.

Fluffy stirred and raised her head. *'Is it that time already?'* she murmured.

'I'm afraid so.'

Fluffy was a strong advocate of napping. She'd take a

nap after breakfast, a mid-morning nap, an after-lunch nap and an evening nap. Shortly after supper she'd settle down for an early night. She said the sea air made her sleepy.

It certainly didn't make the dogs feel sleepy – well, two of them anyway. If I angled one foot in the direction of the path down to the beach, Whippy and Mandy would spring up, raring to go.

Whippy was of British origin. We had first encountered her in the hospital section of a multi-man veterinary practice in East Anglia, where Dave was working as a locum. She was fourteen months old at the time, and had been languishing in hospital for eight months after a collision with a bus. Her right hindleg had been badly fractured and, despite two platings, the bone had refused to knit. Because of the pain and suffering she had experienced and her lengthy hospitalisation, her general condition was very poor when we first saw her. She was extremely thin and had nasty bedsores on both hips, and her tan coat was dull and looked moth-eaten.

When he made enquiries, Dave discovered that her owners had already given permission for her to be euthanased, but due to a conflict of opinion between an elderly receptionist and one of the young vets, this had not been carried out.

With the approval of her owners, Dave and I had offered to take her in and build her up before a third plating was attempted.

As it happened, daily walks in the English countryside and swimming in a nearby river resulted in the bone forming a bridging callus and the third plating was unnecessary. When it was time for us to return to South Africa, Dave approached her owners with the request that we adopt her. Worried that she might be run over again, they agreed and, without further ado, Whippy became a South African citizen.

Presented with one shining example of the benefits of exercise (not having to undergo a third plating), Whippy became a fitness fanatic and when we moved to Dolphin Bay, she informed me that one jog and two walks on the beach each day were simply not enough.

'Being a greyhound, I need to keep fit.'

'In Johannesburg you didn't have a jog and two walks every day.'

'All the more reason,' she explained convincingly. *'I have a lot of catching up to do.'*

'How many walks are we looking at?'

'Ten?' she breathed hopefully.

'TEN! There isn't enough time in a day for ten walks!'

Her face fell. *'What about seven?'*

'Five . . . and not a step further,' I said firmly.

'FIVE walks every day!' she exclaimed happily and rushed off to tell Mandy and Arrow.

'Some of them will be short walks,' I called after her.

I suspected that Whippy's daughter Arrow would be horrified at the news. Arrow was a silver-grey and white greyhound/whippet cross and, at the age of three, she appeared to be in the throes of some strange adolescent phase and spent hours in front of our wardrobe mirror, examining her face for spots. Either that, or she mooched around saying she was bored.

When I attempted to interest her in some form of activity, she'd gaze at me blankly and mutter, *'I don't feel like doing anything, I'm bored.'*

When I pointed out the folly of such an attitude, she'd roll her eyes and saunter off moodily. She tolerated the jog and the two walks but I knew that five walks would definitely take a chunk out of quality mirror time.

Dave's German Shepherd Mandy, who had been his companion before he and I met, would be pleased, but then again she spent most days with him at the surgery.

'It's not that I don't want to be with you and the others,' she explained. *'It's just that he needs the protection.'*

'Protection from what?'

'The patients.'

'Ah,' I nodded.

'I find them generally lacking in discipline.'

'I see.'

'I take them aside in the waiting room, and I tell them: There will be no wriggling, struggling, clawing, hissing, barking or growling in the consulting room. And if you try to BITE, I'll have every tooth from your head when you come out.'

'Do they listen?'

'Oh yes. Fortunately I've never had to resort to threats.'

I stared at her. 'Yes, well, don't worry about us, we'll cope.'

'As long as you understand?'

'I do, I do.'

'Johannes and I are going to enter a mini-marathon,' Dave informed me one morning. 'Would you like to enter too?'

Johannes was Dave's general assistant at the practice. He was in his mid-twenties and of Khoisan descent.

'Me?'

'Yes, it's only fifteen kilometres and we have four weeks in which to train.'

'Thank you, no.'

'Are you sure?'

'Quite sure, thank you.'

The animals and I watched with mild interest as Dave

and Johannes threw themselves into training with a vengeance. Every evening after consulting they would pound the pavements. Sometimes they even pounded the beach. Afterwards Dave would collapse into a chair for the rest of the evening and I took to washing his sweatband on a daily basis.

'Why do they run so slowly?' Whippy asked me one evening.

'What do you mean?'

'Well, if it's a race . . . surely they should be sprinting?'

'I'm sure they will. When they're fit enough.'

Their enthusiasm carried them through the first week, but halfway through the second week the rot set in.

'Aren't you jogging tonight?'

'No.'

'Oh. And Johannes?'

'He says he'll give it a miss tonight.'

After that, apart from sporadic bursts of energy, the training seemed to grind to a halt.

Before we knew it the marathon was upon us. On the Saturday night, I set the alarm for five o'clock the next morning. I had offered to drive Dave and Johannes through to Cougadorp, the neighbouring town where the marathon was being held. When the alarm trilled I woke Dave. Moaning and groaning, he heaved himself out of bed and as he dressed I heard him mumbling. Something about putting in more training.

'It's a bit late for that now,' I called out cheerfully, on my way to rouse Johannes whose bedroom was outside.

I knocked on his door until a muffled groan issued from deep inside and then I went to wake Nic.

Half an hour later, the three of us were sitting in the bakkie waiting for Johannes.

'Maybe he's fallen asleep again.'

'We'd better check.'

As we approached his room the door swung open and a dishevelled Johannes stumbled out. Waves of alcohol fumes washed over us.

'Don't tell me you were partying last night?' I asked horrified. 'How on earth are you going to run a marathon?'

Looking sheepish, Johannes swayed slightly and I noticed that he was barefoot.

'Johannes, where are your shoes?'

'I don't know.'

I turned to Dave. 'You'd better fetch my running shoes.'

As Dave hurried off, I turned back to Johannes, who was wearing tracksuit pants.

'I think you should change into shorts,' I suggested.

'They're in the wash.'

'DAVE, BRING YOUR SPARE SHORTS TOO,' I yelled.

Johannes was short and wiry and my running shoes were two sizes too big. In the end we stuffed them with wads of tissue paper and adjusted the shorts with safety pins to prevent them falling down.

Finally we set off. The fumes were even more noticeable in the close confines of the bakkie and I had severe reservations about Johannes' ability to run the marathon. To me, he appeared not entirely sober.

I dropped the two of them off at the starting point of the race and drove back to the outskirts of town, where I parked on a grass verge. From my vantage point I would be able to see the runners leave town and watch them as they doubled back for the finish. Nic was fast asleep in his safety chair and I sat quietly reading a book. When I glanced up I saw several runners flash by. After a while, I spotted Dave in the middle of a pack, his face bright red. There was no sign of

Johannes. I settled back into my book.

When I looked up again about twenty minutes later, the runners were returning and once more I saw Dave, his teeth clenched and a look of grim determination on his face. But where was Johannes?

The gaps between runners widened and when the last lonely runner stumbled past, I turned on the ignition and drove back to the finishing point. I sat waiting in the bakkie until Dave spotted me and pushed his way through the crowd.

'How did it go?' I asked.

'Fine, fine,' he gasped, leaning against the bakkie. 'But next time I must put in more training.'

'Can we leave now? Where's Johannes?'

'We'll have to wait for the prize-giving.'

'Why? You weren't even near the front.'

'I know. But Johannes was.'

'What!'

Johannes, in his borrowed shoes and borrowed shorts, had come third. Pickled as an onion and with virtually no training, he had sailed past experienced runners. Dedicated runners, who had trained religiously every day for months. As we drove home with a grinning Johannes, I pondered the mysteries of life.

I stepped back and proudly ran my eyes over the flower bed I had just weeded. As I stood admiring my handiwork the bakkie pulled into the long driveway and came to a halt. I wandered over to see Dave emerge with a small white dog in his arms. As he struggled to lock the door, I took the dog from him.

'Whose dog is it?'

'Ours.'

Flenny was a Maltese poodle cross with a curly white coat, a body the shape of a small barrel and warm golden eyes. Dave told me that Mrs Jones, her elderly owner, was moving into a retirement home upcountry, where animals were not allowed. She had asked a friend to bring Flenny to Dave for euthanasia.

'I am not prepared to euthanase her,' Dave protested, as Flenny gazed up at him trustingly. 'Can't another family member give her a home?'

'They have dogs of their own, they don't want her.'

'But she's a lovely dog, surely they can make a plan?'

'They say she's old and arthritic.'

'She's overweight but she doesn't appear to be very old.'

'She's eight.'

'But that's not old!'

'Look Doc, I'm sorry but this has nothing to do with me. I was merely asked to bring the dog in.'

Dave telephoned Mrs Jones and offered to take Flenny.

'She'll never adapt, Doctor, she's too old and spoiled,' the old lady wailed amidst a flood of tears.

'Nonsense, she's not old at all and she will settle if we give her enough time,' he said firmly.

That evening Flenny lay curled up in a blanket on a chair in our sitting room, not a care in the world.

'Look at that,' I said to Dave. 'She's quite settled already.'

'Hmmm.'

The next morning Flenny disappeared. One minute she was outside on the lawn with me, the next minute she was gone. I searched the house and garden frantically before phoning Dave at the surgery.

'Flenny's gone.'

'She must have run back to her old house. I can't get away now, so can you go and fetch her? Mrs Jones is moving out today and I don't want to add to her trauma.'

What about Flenny's trauma, I wondered? Mrs Jones was safe. At least no one was trying to have her put down.

I closed Whippy and Arrow in the house and hurried down the dirt road and up the hill to the post office. Dave had told me that the house was on the hill just above the post office.

Flenny was sitting forlornly on a rubber mat at the front door, waiting patiently for her owner to open it and welcome her back with open arms. When she saw me she sprang up, tail wagging. Relieved that Mrs Jones had not discovered her presence, I scooped her up into my arms and left hastily. Unfortunately I had forgotten to bring a lead and I had to carry her all the way home.

'She'll have to go on a diet,' I told Dave that evening.

The next morning at approximately the same time as the previous day, Flenny went missing again. Fortunately Nic was spending the day with Dave's parents Dodo and Bill, who also lived in Dolphin Bay, and once more I trotted up the hill towards the post office, this time with a lead clutched firmly in my hand.

This morning the house was obviously empty. The windows were curtainless and bags of refuse lay propped up against the garden wall, awaiting removal. Flenny was hunched miserably on the bare cement at the front door. The rubber mat was gone.

When she saw me, she jumped up, barking excitedly. As I looked down at her I felt a pang of sadness for this small fat dog, with her faithful devotion to her owner. An owner who had not cared enough to include Flenny in her plans. I wondered whether we were doing the right thing?

Early the next morning I took her down to the beach for

a walk. She limped and puffed along the sand sniffing at rocks and shells and when I saw that she was tiring, I turned back towards home. That afternoon she managed to evade my watchful eye and slipped off yet again. This time Nic accompanied me and by the time I had dragged a recalcitrant child and a recalcitrant dog all the way home, I was exhausted.

'How much time is enough?' I asked Dave that evening.

At the end of three weeks, Flenny finally accepted that we were her new family. In all, she had returned to her previous home eight times. Once she disappeared when Dave was home and I jumped into the bakkie and sped off in hot pursuit. When I spotted her, she was almost at the post office.

As I drew level, I shouted, 'Flenny, STOP!'

Passers-by gazed on curiously as she put on a burst of speed and covered the last stretch at a gallop.

Gradually the gaps between her disappearances lengthened and three or four days would go by without her making any attempt to slip off.

One morning I sat watching her as she gambolled happily on the grass with the other dogs and, in a flash of understanding, I knew why she had persisted in her efforts to go back home. Dave had told me that Mrs Jones had arranged to be out when Flenny was collected by the friend. Obviously Flenny thought that she had been taken without her owner's knowledge. That it was all a big misunderstanding.

Sadly, this wasn't the case and therein lay a lesson. To me, a rather poignant one.

A few weeks later, as Dave and I were jogging along the beach, I called out to him, 'Look at that!'

Flenny was racing along the waterline, ears streaming

out behind her, her tail reaching for the sky as her feet kicked up spurts of water. Over the weeks she had shed most of her excess weight and, with it, her limp. But even more significant was the joy we sensed in her. She was having a ball!

The Nature of Things

Shortly after Nic's birth, Dave's sister Erica had presented me with a potty. It was powder-blue and made of sturdy plastic.

'Vanessa and Rowan used this very same potty when they were little,' she'd said.

Almost a family heirloom, I thought, a potty that's been around the block a few times.

'Let him get used to seeing it around and when the time comes to use it, he won't feel threatened,' she told me. Which was exactly what I did. With overwhelming success.

From the start Nic loved his potty. Sometimes he would wear it on his head and when we moved to the coast he would insist on taking it down to the beach with him, where he'd use it to build sandcastles. When we collected shells, his would go into the potty and at night, filled with a collection of small cars, it nestled under his bed while he slept.

The trouble started when Erica and Jonathan came down on holiday shortly after I had been diagnosed with systemic lupus, an autoimmune disease in which the body is attacked by its own immune system. I suspect that what followed was a deliberate attempt on God's part to divert my attention. He didn't want me to dwell on the disease.

We all know what an 'Act of God' is. It's an event that strikes out of the blue, often leaving devastation in its wake. And it's not covered by insurance.

'Why is he still in nappies?' asked Erica.

'Well, ummm, you know.'

'Really, Chrystal, it's time he started using his potty.'

'He does use it. Only not for that.'

'That's nonsense. At his age he should be coming out of nappies.'

'Really?'

'Yes, you'll have to actively encourage him.'

Erica was a highly qualified paediatric sister and she knew all about these things. Sometimes I wished that she didn't.

The following morning, I sat Nic down on the sitting room carpet and, crouching down opposite him with the potty squatting happily between us, I explained to him exactly what he was supposed to do in it. He was absolutely horrified! Unable to express himself in words yet (another thing Erica had commented on), his face did it for him. With his eyes bulging in shock and his lips clamped in a thin tight line, he shook his head firmly. 'UH UH.'

I could see his point. His potty was his friend. He loved it. He loved it even more than the wooden trailer Bill had had specially made for him.

'Anyway, just try,' I told him. He gazed back at me, appalled.

The next morning when I dressed him, I left off the nappy.

'When you want to do a wee-wee or a pooh, you must do it in this,' I said, brandishing the potty.

An hour later, Philby came to me in the kitchen where I was busy washing dishes.

'*You'd better come quickly,*' he said officiously, his eyes sparkling with excitement. *'Nic is peeing in his wooden trailer.'*

I found Nic in his bedroom, proudly surveying the trailer, which was awash. Fortunately it had been very well made by an Italian friend of Bill and Dodo's and had not, as yet, sprung a leak. Although my knowledge of potty-training was limited, I recalled reading an article which claimed that the wrong approach to this type of training could lead to psychological problems later in life. Bearing this in mind, I approached the situation with caution.

'That was very clever of you,' I smiled ingratiatingly. 'But next time you must use your potty, OK?'

'Fat chance,' Philby sniggered.

'When I require your input, I'll ask for it,' I glared at him.

No urine or faeces ever sullied the powder-blue interior of that potty. After weeks of sweet-talking, I was forced to conceal the wooden trailer, which remained the prime target of Nic's efforts.

'It's meant for blocks,' I told him.

'I don't see why there should be a problem,' Splittie observed. *'Seafood didn't need any training, she knew what to do from the start.'*

'Well, bully for her,' I said shortly.

'Can't you just let nature take its course?' Whippy asked with a worried frown.

'Not according to Erica.'

Dave and I discussed the matter at length and finally we came to the conclusion that Nic would have to skip potty-training and move straight on to toilet-training.

'Today we're going to learn about toilets,' I informed Nic. He followed me into the toilet and watched curiously as I lifted the toilet seat up and down. Then, I removed the lid of the cistern while he stood on the seat and I showed him what happens to the water when you flush. He was fascinated. He flushed that toilet to within an inch of its life. After thirty minutes, I decided that the orientation process would have to be continued the next day.

Thereafter Nic refused to enter the toilet without a boat; big boats, small boats, speedboats and rowing boats; once or twice, a battery-driven boat. Each day our routine would follow the same pattern. I'd enter first and lift the lid off the cistern, placing it on the floor. Nic would climb up on to the seat and deposit his boats in the water. While he played happily, I'd flush the toilet at intervals, hoping that the sound of gurgling water would elicit the required response. It didn't. He'd chortle delightedly as the boats were sucked to the bottom of the cistern, only to pop up again as it filled.

A week passed, then two. Leaning against the wall one day, watching the water rise in the cistern, I felt my frustration rise in much the same way. Nothing of real substance was being achieved by these rituals. After three weeks, I threw in the toilet roll.

'You'll have to do it,' I told Dave.

'What?'

'Toilet-train Nic.'

'Why?'

'I don't have the right equipment.'

My impatience was exceeded only by my cunning. Over the next few weeks, the dogs, cats and I would watch Dave and Nic disappear into the toilet. We sat together in absolute silence, waiting, as an air of expectancy filled the house. After about twenty minutes they'd emerge, with Nic clasping a boat to his chest and Dave looking harassed. We'd raise our eyebrows enquiringly, only to have Dave shake his head grimly in yet another admission of failure.

Inevitably the thrill of sailing boats in the cistern palled and when this occurred, Nic took matters into his own hands. We should've realised that his peer group consisted of dogs and cats and, not surprisingly, he began to emulate them. When nature called, he would pop out into the garden. As winter approached and venturing outside became a chilly affair, he turned his attention to the toilet. It was a simple matter of convenience really.

In October, our landlady June phoned.

'Chrystal, I just thought I'd let you know that we won't be using the house ourselves this year.'

'Oh wonderful!'

'Instead, we've decided to rent it out as holiday accommodation for one month.'

'Oh.'

We were welcome to rent it at the holiday rates, she told me, but failing this, we would have to vacate the house by the last day of November.

'You'll be able to move back in on the first of January.'

'Thank you.'

'Why couldn't she have just let us stay?' I moaned to Dave.

'Well, she offered to let us stay.'

'Yes, but we can't afford holiday rates.'

'I suppose they need the money.'

'Hmmm.'

To be fair, when we rented the house, it was on the understanding that we would vacate it for a month every December, when June and her family came on holiday. But at the time December had seemed so far away.

Dodo and Bill invited us to spend the month with them and in the second last week of November, with a heavy heart, I began packing. The house was furnished but apart from the furniture, we had to remove everything else. I hated the thought of wiping our presence from it, as if we'd never lived there.

On the day of the move, I scribbled a note to the holiday occupants, asking them to water the plants in the corner of the veranda once a day. I left the note on the kitchen table and with one last wistful look around me, I walked out through the front door.

Fortunately, with the exception of Flenny and Silverkitty, the animals were used to Dodo and Bill's home. Flenny settled in immediately and we kept a watchful eye on Silverkitty for a few days.

We had been staying with Dodo and Bill for a week when Fluffy fell ill. She began sneezing and coughing and within days she went off her food, refusing to eat even a morsel. Dave started her on a course of antibiotics and we waited for her to begin eating again. Two days later she stopped drinking.

'Her respiratory infection is responding to the antibiotics, she should be eating and drinking now,' Dave said, looking worried. 'She's beginning to dehydrate.'

The next day he performed a kidney function test. 'They aren't a hundred per cent,' he said that evening, 'but it doesn't explain her refusal to eat or drink. We'll have to give her fluids.'

When we acquired Fluffy it had not taken us long to discover that she was a cat who was severely resistant to any form of treatment. Even something as simple as deworming. If you attempted to insert anything into her mouth, it immediately triggered a flood of saliva, not unlike the Victoria Falls. Besides this small problem, with typical old-age cunning, she had perfected a technique whereby her four feet functioned independently. They would lash out viciously in several directions at once and while this was happening, her body would tie itself into knots. Fluffy was not an easy cat to treat. Getting the antibiotics into her had been a major endeavour, and now a drip! I stared at Dave in dismay.

'I'll run it straight into her abdomen,' he said. 'You'll have to hold her with her stomach facing upwards.'

'Dave, it's not going to be so easy . . .'

'Nobody said it would be easy,' he snapped. 'But it has to be done. She'll never tolerate an intravenous drip and this is our only alternative.'

We decided to use the kitchen table and as I attempted to immobilise her body, she fought me tooth and nail. Literally.

'Hold her head.'

'I am holding her head.'

'Hold it more firmly, I cannot get this needle in while she's trying to bite me.'

'OK, now I've got it.'

'Get her back feet too.'

'I can't, I've got her front feet. I only have two hands.'

'This is hopeless,' he exclaimed, throwing his hands in the air.

Dave tended towards the dramatic whenever one of our own animals needed treatment, I had noticed.

'I'M DOING THE BEST I CAN,' I shrieked.

Eventually we managed to get the required amount of fluid into her. Afterwards, we carried her, almost in a state of collapse, to her basket in a corner of our bedroom. We retired to the sitting room, emotionally drained and barely on speaking terms and sat silently dabbing at our wounds and sipping neat whisky at intervals.

The performance was repeated the next night and the

night after that. On the fourth night Dave turned to me, perspiration dripping from his face,

'Chrystal, I think we have to accept that Fluffy has decided to die. It's not fair to go on traumatising her in this way.'

'She's not ready to die.'

'Love, maybe it's just her time.'

'It's not her time.'

'How can you know that?'

'I know.'

'Well, I'm not prepared to traumatise her any further. Tonight is the last time.'

Early the next morning, I watched as he set off for the surgery. When the bakkie had disappeared around the corner, I went into the kitchen. I took an egg from the fridge and broke it into a bowl, added milk and whisked it for a few seconds.

'What are you making?' asked Bill. 'An omelette?'

'No, an egg-flip,' I replied, tipping in a spoonful of glucose.

I carried the bowl, a syringe and two thick towels into the bedroom. Fluffy lay back in her basket watching me wearily, as I placed the items on the carpet next to her.

Fifteen minutes later, I had succeeded in wrapping her up like an Eskimo, with only her head poking out of the tightly wound towels. Her orange eyes glared resentfully as I dripped egg-flip into her mouth.

'I'm sorry, I'm not allowing you to die,' I told her.

A few hours later I repeated the procedure.

Later that afternoon, I did it again and this time I noticed that her struggles had diminished slightly. She almost appeared to be enjoying the egg-flip.

The next morning after Dave had left, I entered the bedroom, carrying a saucer filled with egg-flip. I placed the saucer in front of her and said calmly: 'You can do this on your own, or we can do it together.'

Never was a threat less veiled. She stared into my eyes for a long moment and then, with a deep sigh, she lowered her head and began lapping from the saucer. Fluffy had decided that it was easier to live.

'I told you it wasn't her time,' I remarked that evening, as we watched her devour a bowl of minced pilchards.

'Hmmm,' Dave murmured, glancing at me speculatively.

Over the next few days she went from strength to strength and when the weekend arrived, Dave suggested that we camp out on the Saturday night. He said we needed to de-stress.

Not wanting to expose Nic to mosquitoes and the possible risk of snakes, we left him behind with Dodo and Bill and at five o'clock on the Saturday afternoon, we set off. Mandy, Whippy and Arrow travelled in the back of the bakkie while Flenny sat in front with us.

Dolphin Bay lay between two rivers, the Tunny river in the east and the Hippo river in the west. The Hippo river was twenty minutes' drive from the centre of town along a twisting, unevenly tarred road lined by pastures and thick low bushveld. A troop of vervet monkeys inhabited the bushveld and often gathered at the side of the road to stare at passing vehicles.

A few kilometres from town the road snaked through a small hamlet of scattered houses down to the banks of the river. Here a rough causeway of rock and gravel, only wide enough to take one vehicle at a time, had been constructed across the river. When it rained heavily, the causeway was often totally submerged, cutting off access to the handful of houses on the other side.

We crossed the causeway and drove on to a potholed dirt

road. Beyond the houses, the road wended its way past dense bush and areas of marshland dotted with clumps of bright yellow, blue and purple veld flowers.

Three kilometres further on, the road doubled back slightly and curved up over a hill. To our right as we crested the hill large bush-covered dunes tumbled down from the road to the beach below, where a vista of silvery sand and endless blue sea lay stretched out before us. Just before the dunes began, a narrow grassy track veered off into the bush to a small clearing set amidst a grove of milkwood and black wattle trees.

Dave turned on to the track and brought the bakkie to a halt and while he opened the canopy to let the other three out, I lifted Flenny down. As her paws touched the ground she bounced off happily down the path, sniffing the grass and bushes excitedly. Mandy, Whippy and Arrow zoomed past, almost flattening her in their haste to explore and, responding to the challenge, she hurtled after them. Who would have thought she would become such an outdoor enthusiast, I marvelled, remembering the cosseted overweight dog Dave had brought home. Given half the chance she would hike mountain trails, I thought. Equipped with a Swiss Army knife and a box of matches.

'Shall we unpack the food and sleeping bags now, or go for a swim first?' Dave asked, coming up behind me.

'Let's unpack and gather wood for the fire before we swim. Then we don't have to hurry back before it gets dark.'

While Dave unloaded the food and sleeping bags, I wandered off through the trees, along a black sandy path criss-crossed at intervals by buck spoor. I stooped to pick up pieces of bark and dry wood from the ground, breathing in the fragrant smell of bush and decaying vegetation. As the setting sun sent its last weak shafts of sunlight through the

tops of the trees, my mind drifted back to Swaziland and the forest.

Suddenly, the stillness was shattered by high-pitched shrieks coming from the direction of the clearing.

When I arrived on the scene, Dave was already there. Arrow was leaping around yelping frantically, a porcupine quill dangling from the middle of her nose.

'You silly girl!' I giggled. 'You mustn't sniff porcupines.'

'*But I sniff EVERYTHING*,' she howled, as Dave gripped her snout and plucked the quill from her nose.

'The apple doesn't fall far from the tree,' I observed cynically. Whippy pretended not to hear.

After we'd stacked the wood in a circle of stones, we made our way through low tunnels formed by overhanging trees and bush. It was already dusk and the sea sand was cool under our feet. At the top of a steep sand dune I paused for a moment and then leapt out into space, plummeting through the air to land several metres lower down, my legs sinking into the shifting sand. As I leapt again, I heard Dave give a loud 'Whoop' as he launched himself after me.

We brushed the sand from our clothes and strolled across the beach towards the water. The dogs raced ahead and, at the high-water mark, white waves frothed on to the shore, forming pools in their pawprints.

We flung our clothing on the dry sand and plunged into the turquoise waves, floating gently to and fro, the warm silky water caressing our skins. Mandy floated alongside us, while Whippy and Arrow chased each other madly across the shallows, skittering through the water, sending plumes of spray high into the air. With her short legs, Flenny was at a distinct disadvantage in the sea and each time she attempted to swim out to us, the waves would gather her up and sweep her back on to the shore. Eventually, in disgust, she gave up trying and trotted off along the waterline, sniffing at shells and heaps of seaweed.

When we finally emerged from the water feeling tingly and relaxed, darkness had fallen and the beach was illuminated by a soft pale moon suspended above the dunes. Dave opened the bottle of wine he had brought with him and as we sat sipping wine from plastic tumblers, the seawater dried on our skins, leaving them taut and salty. The dogs sprawled around us as we sat gazing out to sea, too lazy to speak. And as we gazed, the sea began to glow with a soft green radiance.

'It's phosphorescence,' Dave murmured.

Shimmering waves swirled and broke, as if someone up there had strewn liquid stardust over the water. Later, we entered the water again, laughing at the sight of four dogs aglow with sea-glitter. In the shallows, shoals of tiny luminous fish scurried before our feet, minute torches of the deep. The dogs peered down at the fish, totally bemused.

Eventually hunger pangs forced us back up through the dunes and while Dave got the fire going, I prepared the food. When the fire was ready we sat around the glowing coals, breathing in the delicious smell of sizzling sausages.

'*I like mine rare,*' Whippy whispered anxiously.

'Don't worry, it won't be long now.'

After supper, we settled the dogs down on blankets in the back of the bakkie, afraid that they might wander off during the night. Dave doused the fire and I lay back in my sleeping-bag, gazing up at the stars and remembering an incident that had happened years before, when I was thirteen.

'Your father and I have decided that it's time to go on another camping holiday,' my mother announced one evening. It was important for us to get back to nature, she said, and it wouldn't cost the earth.

I loved camping, but my enthusiasm was marred by memories of previous camping experiences. That, and a deep suspicion that Nature had no desire for us to get back to it.

Not being regular campers, we did not own a tent. Nor did we possess any of the other equipment usually required, such as camping beds, sleeping bags, gas lights, and so on. This was easily remedied because my mother's brother John was a scout master and camping fanatic and he could lend us everything we needed. Which was fine. In theory.

In practice, my mother and father would spend up to four hours in the heat of the day arguing about how to put up the tent. It was always a different tent. We never got to use the same tent twice. After the first hour, my mother would accuse my father of leaving a bag of poles behind at home.

'John, I'm sure there were two bags of poles,' she would insist, tendrils of hair plastered on to her head as her perm wilted under the baking sun.

'Fay, there was only the one bag,' he'd snap irritably, his face the colour of a boiled lobster.

Inevitably, when the tent was halfway up, they would discover that the pole needed for the bottom, had been used for the roof and the whole thing would have to be dismantled. At an early age I realised that offering to help was not a good idea. They would give me conflicting instructions and when the tent collapsed during the night, I would be blamed.

On this particular occasion, my Uncle John had suggested that we camp on the banks of the Hippo river. There were no houses there in those days and an area had been cleared next to the river for camping purposes.

'It's paradise,' he said. 'The bird life is incredible and you wake in the morning to the sound of birdsong and water lapping on the banks of the river.'

I was allowed to invite my best friend Colleen, and because there were four of us my Uncle John supplied us with two small tents. When he dropped the tents and other equipment off at our home, he spent an hour coaching my mom and dad on how to erect them. They understood perfectly, they assured him.

'Piece of cake,' said my dad.

We arrived at the camp site at about ten o'clock the next morning. A wind had come up during the night and a pall of black dust hung over the freshly cleared area. Several other tents and a couple of caravans were already in place.

My dad selected a spot close to a thicket of milkwood trees and while he and my mother wrestled with their tent, Colleen and I erected ours. When it was up, we assembled the two camping beds and placed them inside the tent. We went back to the car for the sleeping bags and pillows and when we re-entered the tent, I noticed a bulge in the canvas of my camping bed. The beds were very shallow, the canvas suspended just above the ground. I dropped the bedding on the ground and squatting down, I reached out to smooth the bulge. As I ran my hand across it, I realised that the bulge was solid. And then it moved.

I stood up and looked down at the bed thoughtfully.

'Colleen.'

'Yes?'

'There's something under my bed.'

'What?'

'I don't know. It moved when I touched it.'

'Well, lift the bed and look.'

The Nature of Things

I bent over, grasped the frame of the bed and lifted it. As I did so, a long black snake slithered out. It shot between my feet and headed for the opening of the tent.

Startled by our synchronised screams, my father came running.

'What's happening, what's happening?' he asked as my mother rushed up behind him.

'A SNAKE! Under the camping bed!' Colleen gibbered.

'I don't see it, where is it now?'

'It's gone,' I said. 'It went out through the opening.'

Without uttering a word, my mother ran to the car, jumped in, slammed the doors and began rolling up the windows. She had a pathological fear of snakes. In fact, of all reptiles because she didn't care much for lizards either.

It took my father almost two hours to persuade my mother to leave the car.

'Fay, I promise you it's gone. There's no sign of it.'

'Have you checked our tent?'

'I've checked everything. You can't spend the rest of the holiday in the car.'

From where I was standing, the expression on her face seemed to dispute this. Eventually, in desperation, my father pointed out that vehicles are not snake-proof. He went on to relate a story about an acquaintance who was driving happily along when he noticed a puff adder sloughing out below the dashboard.

My mother didn't even wait for my father to finish his story. The car door jerked open and she said she needed to use the toilet facilities very urgently. Colleen and I trotted across the clearing with her, to the two little wooden sheds standing side by side at the edge of the trees. One shed was for men and the other for women. We had inspected them briefly earlier. They were very basic inside, containing a wooden box-like structure with a hole for a seat, positioned over a deep pit.

As we approached the sheds, the door of one burst open and a stout, blonde-haired woman shot out, her shorts around her ankles.

'WHATEVER YOU DO, DON'T GO IN THERE!' she yelled in an American accent.

Before we could ask her what was going on, she heaved up her shorts and raced across the clearing towards a white caravan.

Completely mystified, we stared after her. She disappeared into the caravan but within seconds she was out again, brandishing a lethal-looking pistol in her right hand. By this time a crowd was gathering. Shouting, 'STAND BACK!' she kicked open the door of the shed and stepped inside. As we watched, one gunshot after another rocked the little structure. Finally, there was a brief silence and she emerged into the sunlight, the pistol still smoking in her hand.

'That's one dead snake!' she snorted triumphantly.

Apparently she had gone to use the toilet and had no sooner ensconced herself on the wooden platform when she heard a rustling sound coming from beneath her. She stood up and peered into the pit and as her eyes became accustomed to the gloom, she spotted a large black snake. It was busy curling itself up on the ledge where the wooden box rested on the ground.

I felt very sorry for the snake, obviously the same one that had been under my camping bed. It was a night adder, they said.

'Dad, why couldn't she just have left the snake in peace?' I complained.

'Chrystal, what if it had bitten someone on the backside?

It's not as if one can apply a tourniquet.'

After this incident, my mother refused point-blank to use the facilities and we watched her disappear into the thick bush carrying a toilet roll. My father said she was taking a hell of a chance. According to the law of averages, he said, she was far more likely to encounter a snake in the bush than in a wooden privy. When I asked him why a snake had in fact been found in the privy, he said that was the other law. Murphy's one.

That night a gale-force wind struck the camping site. Despite this, Colleen and I slept well and our tent withstood the onslaught. My mother and father were not so lucky. They awoke from dreams of being suffocated, to find themselves buried under a heap of canvas. The noise of the howling wind had drowned out their cries for help and my dad said they battled for some time before they managed to get out. Apparently, by the time they did, my mother was in quite a state.

In addition to her fear of reptiles, she suffered from claustrophobia and she promptly added collapsed tents to her list of lifts and other confined spaces to be avoided. My dad said that was silly, because no one would knowingly try to enter a collapsed tent.

When we awoke on the morning of the third day it was drizzling steadily and overnight the campsite had been transformed into a morass of runny black mud. When my dad emerged from his tent for breakfast, he paused and silently surveyed the scene. Then he uttered two words.

'Paradise Lost,' he said.

It took us only thirty minutes to pack.

When I opened my eyes again it was dawn. The sky was overcast, dark clouds scudding overhead. Out of the corner of my eye I sensed movement and glancing towards the edge of the clearing I saw a small buck silhouetted in the cold dawn light. I lay dead still as it stepped forward towards the fire. The remains of our salad lay on a plate next to the cold ashes and it sniffed at the plate delicately. As I watched, it began to nibble at a lettuce leaf and then a carrot. Every few seconds its eyes flicked nervously in our direction and I tried not to blink. When the plate was empty, it turned and silently melted back into the thicket. One minute it was there, the next minute it was gone.

By the time Dave awoke, I had a pot of water boiling on the flames and after coffee we went for a long walk along the network of dirt roads. The bush and long grass on either side of the road were alive with spiderwebs, spun in silk and dew. Now and again, a bird call pierced the blanket of silence the dull sky had cast over the day.

Then it was time to leave. Dave had to be back for Sunday morning consulting. Leaving our euphoria lying crumpled next to the ashes of the dead fire, we drove back into town.

Two days before we were due to move back into the sea-house, Silverkitty disappeared. I searched the area around the dam and all the adjoining gardens but found no trace of him. It was as if he had disappeared into thin air. Worried, I phoned Dave at the surgery and on his way home that afternoon he stopped in at the sea-house. The holiday occupants hadn't seen Silverkitty. As Dave was leaving, they told him that they would be departing very early the next morning, a day earlier than expected. They were hoping to miss the New Year traffic on the roads.

Thrilled at the news, we began packing immediately and at eight o'clock the next morning we pulled into the long driveway. As we climbed the steps up on to the veranda, I noticed a note pinned to the front door.

'Silverkitty arrived just after midnight.'

The plants in the corner of the veranda were shrivelled and dry and I rushed inside to find the watering can. As the last drop of water dripped from the can, I swung around to re-enter the dining room. Sitting in a row watching me were Carrots, Philby and Silverkitty.

I eyed Silverkitty thoughtfully. Was it coincidence that he had made his way back to the house, to arrive a mere few hours before we did? Why did I have this overwhelming feeling that somehow he had known that the people were leaving a day early.

'Now you're being ridiculous,' I muttered to myself.

Splitting Up

It was marvellous to be back in the sea-house again and the dogs and I promptly resumed our early morning jogs on the beach. Sometimes we would see buck spoor in the sand leading from the bushy dunes down to the sea and back again. What did they do in the sea, I wondered? Surely they weren't drinking the salt water?

'They eat the seaweed,' Dave told me.

On a few occasions we startled small buck standing on the smooth sand below the dunes. Upon seeing us, they would flit silently back into the thick bush, like elusive shadows.

'Leave,' I'd say quietly to the dogs and they did.

They seemed to share my feeling of wonder at living in this place, where seagulls and fish eagles wheeled overhead and wild creatures led secret lives in the dunes. There was a sense of harmony, of being at peace with our surroundings and the creatures who shared it with us.

'Dave, I think Splittie is sick.'
'Why?'

Splitting Up

'She's been eating less the past few days and tonight she hasn't touched her food.'

We stared at the full saucer on the kitchen table. Something was wrong. Normally Splittie approached every meal as if it was her last, licking and polishing the bowl until not a speck remained. This was a throwback to the days when she had survived by foraging for scraps on the Natal south coast.

'Where is she now?'

'On the couch in the sitting room. She's been sleeping a lot lately.'

Dave knelt down beside the couch and Splittie raised her head and looked at him suspiciously. She lay still as he ran his hands over her body, but when he palpated her abdomen she gave a squeak of pain and he paused for a moment to stroke her. When he attempted it a second time, she tried to move away.

'There's something there,' he murmured thoughtfully.

'What?'

'I can feel a hard mass in her abdomen.'

'What do you think it is?'

'I'm not sure. It could be a hairball or something more serious.'

'What do you mean?'

'A tumour.'

I stared at him, aghast.

'Look, don't let's overreact. I'll take her in tomorrow and do an X-ray.'

The next morning Dave set off with Splittie at his side. As I watched the bakkie reverse down the long driveway I felt a gnawing worry settle in my own stomach.

One hour later he phoned.

'The X-ray shows a large mass. I'm going to do a laparotomy

and see what it is. It's too big for a hairball.'

'When will you start?'

'Almost immediately, as soon as Johannes has sterilised the drapes and instruments.'

'Will you phone me when you know?'

'Yes.'

My attempts at housework that morning were interspersed with periods of standing still, staring mindlessly into space.

A few hours later the telephone rang.

'It's cancer.'

'Oh no.'

'I've removed as much as I could but it was extensive and may have already metastasised to the lungs. She's very weak.'

'Oh.'

'Chrystal, I'm afraid the long-term prognosis is not very promising and, to be honest, I have my doubts as to whether she will survive post-op. At the moment her condition is critical.'

Leaving Nic with Dodo and Bill, I spent the afternoon sitting on the floor next to Splittie's cage. She was semi-conscious and on a drip. At intervals she would stir and whimper weakly and I'd reach out and stroke her gently, until she was still. As I sat watching her, it struck me afresh how small she was for an adult cat. My thoughts returned to the day when I had first seen her truculent little face glaring up at me from a cardboard box.

Unlike Philby, who had conned his way into our hearts, Splittie had simply kicked the doors down, marched in and started giving orders. Small and stunted though she was, she had the spirit of a lioness.

When consulting was over, I cradled her in my arms while

Splitting Up

Dave carried the drip and we took her home. We settled her down on cushions in the middle of our bed and took turns watching over her through the night.

In the last hour of darkness before dawn, her eyelids lifted wearily and she gazed into my eyes for a long moment, as if trying to tell me something.

'Don't worry, we'll take good care of Seafood,' I whispered and her eyelids drooped shut. A few minutes later, she gave one last deep sigh and stopped breathing.

We buried her under the old tree aloe just below the veranda.

Whippy and Philby sat next to me on the steps as Dave dug the small hole.

'She wasn't nearly as hard-boiled as she tried to make out,' Whippy observed sadly.

'No,' I said, tears streaming down my face.

'Well, she wasn't always very nice,' said Philby.

'*Nice* was not a word she cared to dwell upon.'

Splittie's death left a gap in our lives. The kind of gap that is never really filled.

A few days later, I was busy making sandwiches at lunchtime when I heard Dave arrive. I glanced up as he entered the kitchen. He was carrying a Siamese cat in his arms. Breadknife poised in mid-air, I stared at the cat.

'Whose cat is it?'

'She belongs to Mrs Holmes. She's coming to board with us for a week.'

'Oh.'

'I offered to let her stay in our spare bedroom.'

'Mrs Holmes?'

'No, the cat. She's nineteen years old and doesn't like being in a cage.'

'What's her name?'

'Gemini. Chrystal, will you close her in the spare bedroom while I fetch her things from the bakkie?'

'OK.' I took the cat from him.

Gemini sniffed around the room in a relaxed manner, completely unfazed by her new surroundings. She was in excellent condition for a nineteen-year-old cat. I wondered what Mrs Holmes was feeding her. As I left the room, I bumped into Dave, who was carrying two large cat baskets, a litter tray, two cushions, two blankets and several plastic packets.

'Here, let me help you,' I offered, as he stumbled and almost fell.

'There are a few more things in the bakkie,' he muttered, dropping the baskets and litter tray on the floor. Taking the packets from him, I unpacked the contents on to the kitchen table.

The first packet contained three packs of fillet steak. It was ages since we'd eaten steak, I thought, thrilled at the sight. The second packet contained a dozen eggs and seven gem squashes, while the third was filled with a variety of saucers and bowls.

'This is wonderful, we can have steak and eggs for supper,' I called out enthusiastically as Dave walked in, carrying two more cushions, another litter tray, two crocheted blankets and a large bag of cat litter.

'It's not for us, it's for Gemini,' he said, handing me two foolscap pages. 'These are the instructions.'

For breakfast, Gemini was to be given a saucerful of fresh milk and half a freshly boiled gem squash mixed with a tittup of butter. Lunch comprised grilled fillet steak cut into small pieces and a bowl of fresh water. Supper was a scrambled egg and the other half of the gem squash, freshly boiled. The instructions regarding meals – times, preparation and presentation – filled one page. The second page dealt with more mundane matters – the changing of her bedding; the changing of her litter tray (twice a day); toys, the use of, and daily grooming.

It was an extremely busy week.

'Will you hold this ladder while I change the light bulb?' Dave called out to me.

'Not now, I'm busy.'

'Doing what?'

'Cooking Gem Squash's lunch.'

'The cat's name is GEMINI!'

'Sorry.'

'Why don't we ever get steak?' moaned Carrots, a string of saliva dangling from his chin, as the aroma of grilled fillet wafted through the kitchen.

'It's because we're not pedigreed,' Philby informed him.

'Nonsense! It's because we can't afford steak,' I explained, sniffing the air appreciatively.

Despite the time and effort involved, at the end of the week I was sad to see Gemini leave. She was a delightful cat and she deserved every luxury lavished upon her. It would be nice to have a Siamese again, I reflected wistfully.

'This is Percy,' Dave said, placing a cardboard box on the kitchen floor. As he opened the flaps, a penguin's head popped up and gazed at me with interest.

'Hello, Percy.'

'I thought we'd let him roam the garden as we did with Parker.'

Percy was a strong, healthy-looking juvenile. It wouldn't be long before he was off to sea. He seemed to be constantly hungry and, once he had established the source of the fish, he took to spending hours staring up at the fridge with bright hopeful eyes. Willing it to open and release its contents.

One afternoon, bearing a bowl of pilchards, I strolled out on to the lawn.

'Percy,' I called. There was no sign of him. This was strange. Usually he was ready and waiting. Then I spotted him lying in a corner of the veranda under an old wooden table. I knelt down and peered at him.

'Percy,' I said.

He raised his head slightly and shook it, making no effort to stand. Reaching in under the table, I lifted him out. I examined him carefully but everything appeared perfectly normal, apart from a slight swelling above one eye. Just then, Dave arrived home.

'Dave, there's something wrong with Percy.'

'What's wrong?'

'There's a slight swelling above one eye and he seems a bit disorientated.'

Dave squatted down next to me.

'Hmmm, there *is* a swelling, I wonder what could've caused it?'

My eyes strayed to a luminous green golf ball lying on the lawn and I recalled seeing Nic tossing it for Whippy earlier that afternoon.

'NIC!' I yelled and he came running from his bedroom.

'When you were throwing the ball for Whippy, did it hit Percy?'

Nic gazed up at me with big innocent blue eyes. Too big and innocent, I thought, regarding him suspiciously.

'Chrystal, the child can barely string two words together, how do you expect him to confess?'

'He can nod his head,' I said, looking at Nic, whose head

remained immobile.

Percy would not take any fish that night, nor the next morning. In the afternoon, I opened his beak and pushed a sliver of fish down his throat. He promptly vomited it up and in the two days that followed I was unable to get him to keep anything down.

'What are we going to do?' I asked Dave. 'He can't even stand upright.'

That evening Dave phoned the same zoologist he had consulted before. The zoologist said he could be of very little assistance. It was more of a veterinary problem and beyond his sphere of experience. Towards the end of the conversation, he mentioned hearing that sick or weak penguins could be tube-fed directly into the stomach. It would involve passing a tube down the bird's throat into its stomach and running fluids in through the tube.

Dave replaced the receiver, looking thoughtful.

'He says we might be able to tube-feed Percy.'

'With what?'

'Perhaps an electrolyte solution or something more nutritional.'

'Wouldn't it be easier just to run some drip in under the skin of his neck?'

'It might be easier, but we haven't always had much success with that method. Sometimes it seems to cause air-sac problems and we lose them, especially the weaker birds.'

'Percy is looking quite weak.'

'Yes, he's dehydrating. I think we should try tube-feeding.'

Dave nipped off to the surgery and returned with a 60ml syringe and a length of latex tubing. Discarding the plunger, he attached the tubing to the syringe nozzle. I held Percy while Dave opened his beak and inserted the tubing into his

Splitting Up

mouth.

'Hang on, I think it needs some lubrication,' he said, and went to fetch the lubrigel from his black bag.

'This is better,' he said, as the tube slid smoothly down Percy's throat.

'Look, you can see the opening to his windpipe here at the back of his tongue. The tube has to pass over the opening or the fluid will run into his lungs.'

When approximately 20 centimetres of tubing had disappeared down Percy's throat, Dave paused and blocked the tubing with a kink. He held the syringe up, while I poured the warmed electrolyte solution into the open end, where the plunger would normally go. When the solution reached the 40ml mark, he said, 'OK, I think that's enough to start with.'

I elevated the syringe slightly and Dave released the kink, allowing the solution to flow. Within seconds the syringe was empty and Percy burped loudly as Dave removed the tubing.

'Let's see how he does. We can give him some more in a few hours.'

We lay Percy down in his crate on a hot-water bottle and an hour later when I checked, he seemed a bit brighter. By bedtime we had tubed him three times.

The next morning, I awoke early and crept quietly from the bed, trying not to disturb Dave. I tiptoed through to the sitting room where Percy's crate squatted in a corner. Slowly, afraid of what I might find, I lifted the towel covering the crate. Percy was lying on his stomach. He was very still.

'Oh no, he's dead,' I mumbled and reached out to touch him. As he felt my touch, he lifted his head and stood up.

'DAVE, DAVE!' I shrieked. 'Percy's standing!'

A day later, we replaced the electrolyte solution with a

non-dairy nutritional mixture used in the feeding of invalids. Before long, Percy was swallowing slivers of fish and then whole fish again.

We concluded that he must have been suffering from concussion and I had a serious word with Nic and Whippy regarding the reckless use of luminous green golf balls. Only Whippy had the grace to look embarrassed.

A few weeks later, Percy went off to sea. This incident taught us something of great value in the treatment of penguins. From then on, we began tubing weak and dehydrated penguins upon admission.

'I wish Nic would start speaking now,' I said to Dave one morning. 'Erica and Jonathan are coming down on holiday soon.'

'Chrystal, he'll speak when he's ready.'

From an early age, Nic could say 'Mom' or 'Dad' but when we tried to encourage him to expand his vocabulary, he would clamp his lips together stubbornly.

Shortly after the 'Percy' incident, a client who lived just up the hill from the surgery brought in a cross-Siamese stray. She said that they were unable to keep it themselves as her husband was allergic to cats and Dave decided that the surgery needed a cat.

Nic took one look at the cat and, in a very clear voice, he said: 'Be-barp.'

We stared at him.

'What did you say?' I asked.

'Be-barp,' he stated firmly.

We decided to name the cat Be-barp.

After this, Nic's vocabulary took off with a vengeance

and before long he was using phrases like 'an unfortunate victim of circumstances' and 'innocent until proven guilty'.

Once again we were forced to accept that we could set up goalposts until the cows came home. Nic would only kick the ball when he was ready.

On Foreign Shores

After Splittie's death, the summer somehow seemed to lose its sparkle and that year winter arrived early. And with a vengeance.

From early April gale-force winds battered the house, causing the metal window and door frames to rattle noisily in protest. The wind snuck in under the roofing, shrieking through the sitting room which did not have a ceiling, making normal conversation impossible at times. For days on end rain poured steadily down, teaming up with the wind to lash against walls, windows and doors, seeking entry. Beads of moisture formed on the inside of the glass panes, melting together to send rivulets of water trickling down the walls. Sometimes the house would shudder as mountainous waves exploded on the shore.

Of course the old house had seen it all before and, with a resigned sigh, it seemed to hunker down more deeply into the hollow, stubbornly resisting the onslaught. In the bay, fishing boats and trawlers were tossed around by thrashing seas and it was hard to conceive that conditions must be worse beyond the bay. I often wondered where Parker and Percy were.

The silky, spun-gold beaches of summer underwent a

startling transformation as huge tree trunks were flung from the sea on to the sand like so many matchsticks. Scattered amongst them, we found smooth lengths of exquisitely carved driftwood. Sea sculptures. The sand on the beach was sucked back into the heaving sea, leaving outcrops of dark rock where we had never seen rock before. Almost overnight, massive banks of purple, brown and green seaweed piled up on the beach, filling the air with a sharp iodine smell.

Sometimes in the mornings, as the dogs and I sped along the waterline, the wind would hurl handfuls of brown scummy foam after us. The foam clung to my skin and the dogs' fur and after the run we'd stagger breathlessly up the path covered in wisps of sticky brown slime. Like candyfloss gone wrong.

We missed Splittie so much, but in a way our grief found expression in the turbulence of the elements and was soothed. Nature's lifeforce seething all around us brought with it an acceptance of death. A sort of acceptance.

I had half-expected Seafood's subdued personality to blossom after Splittie's death, but it remained more or less unchanged.

'She's been repressed for too long,' Philby observed sagely. *'She's always going to be wishy-washy.'*

'There are one or two other cats who could do with a bit of repression,' I responded with a meaningful look.

'What is repression?' asked Carrots.

'You should know, it's . . .'

'PHILBY!'

He looked hurt. *'I was only trying to say . . .'*

'Never mind what you were trying to say.'

'Do you receive income from any other source?' the accountant asked, staring down at the sheet of figures in his hand.

'No.'

Now that Dave was running his own practice, he was required to submit an annual Tax Return, which included a Balance Sheet and Statement of Income and Expenditure. Dodo suggested that we enlist the services of a local accountant, which we did. I supplied him with the necessary information and paperwork and, with commendable speed, he drew up the required documentation. But he didn't appear to be too happy about it.

'I'll have to find a job,' I told Dave that evening.

'Why?'

'Because I think the accountant feels sorry for us.'

Shortly after this Dodo informed me that the local librarian was retiring after seventeen years in the post.

'You have library experience, don't you?'

'Yes, but I'm not a qualified librarian.'

'Neither is she.'

'Oh.'

Upon leaving school I had been employed as a library assistant at the public library in my hometown. At the time I had seriously considered studying for the necessary degree, but when I did leave to attend university, it was to enrol for a BSc degree with the intention of studying veterinary science. My fascination for books was exceeded only by my love of animals. Unfortunately this love of animals was not enhanced by a scientific mind and an ongoing clash with physics caused me to drop out. Newton and I were not destined to be soulmates.

'I think you should get an application form from the municipality,' Dodo said.

The library was situated in an old house overlooking the

beachfront. Several of the interior walls had been removed to accommodate bookshelves. As a regular user I had found the adult section fairly adequate, but I had noted that the children's section was severely limited in both space and variety. A large oval table and an unwieldy wooden stand containing records were pushed up against shelves of children's books, hampering easy access. A sign displayed on the outer wall of the building stated that children were only permitted to use the library on two afternoons per week.

I duly submitted the application form and four weeks went by without any response. Then one morning the telephone rang and it was Mr Haig, the town clerk.

'Will you be able to come in for an interview tomorrow morning?' he asked. He informed me that the interview would be conducted in the council chamber at eleven o'clock.

Why the council chamber, I wondered, feeling slightly overwhelmed.

The following morning when I took my seat at the head of a very long table, I understood. Seated around the table was the entire Library Committee (eight members), two town councillors, the town clerk and the mayor. I was being interviewed by twelve people.

Trying to control my quaking knees, I answered the questions being fired at me from all sides. Finally a silence fell and I sat quietly, waiting for them to signal that the interview was at an end. The chairman of the Library Committee, an elderly gentleman with the red-faced authoritarian look of an army colonel, cleared his throat and asked: 'If your application is successful, what would be your first priority?'

I stared at him thoughtfully for a moment, considering the question. 'My first priority,' I said slowly, 'would be the children. I would like to do more for the children.'

The chairman beamed at me and nodded. 'Thank you. I think that will be all.'

A few days later, Mr Haig phoned to inform me that the post was mine. I would work with the current librarian for the first two weeks and after that I would be on my own.

Nic was two years and eight months old when I started working at the library. Three months prior to that we had enrolled him at a local playschool for two days a week. He was not terribly enamoured of this, but we felt that as an only child he needed the company of other children. He could not go on regarding dogs and cats as his only peer group for the rest of his life. Now he would attend the playschool every morning and spend his afternoons with Dodo and Bill.

Mrs Prentis was a short, thin woman in her early seventies. With hindsight, I should've realised that after seventeen years she would find it very difficult to relinquish her position. This only came to me much later and the first week was a baptism of boredom. For a week I sat at the oval table watching her work.

'Can't I help you with that?'

'No, no, it's quicker if I do it myself.'

'Isn't there anything else I can do?'

'Don't worry, you sit and relax.'

'Shall I check the shelves to see if the books are in order?' I asked desperately.

'No, don't bother, you know what the public are like, they'll just mix them up again.'

On the third day Dave entered our bedroom at lunchtime to find me kneeling on the floor with my head resting on the bed.

'What on earth are you doing?'

'I'm praying.'

'For what?'

'For the strength to get me through this day.'

I went to see Mr Haig and explained to him that my previous library experience had not included certain administrative and statistical reports, which had been dealt with solely by the chief librarian and assistant librarian.

Public libraries in most small towns are linked to the provincial library services. While the buildings, furniture and staff are supplied by the municipalities themselves, the book stock and stationery are supplied by the provincial library services. In return, they require ongoing statistical information and reports.

'I need to know what these involve,' I told Mr Haig.

My second week was spent at a public library in a neighbouring town learning the intricacies of the administration system from the librarian there.

Mrs Prentis was rather annoyed when she learned of this plan. 'Why do you have to go there?' she asked, looking offended. 'I can teach you everything you need to know.'

'I have no idea,' I lied, lolling back in a chair as she bustled around busily.

At the start of the third week, early on the Monday morning, I unlocked the front door of the library and stepped inside. I stood for a moment, absorbing the peaceful stillness of the books. Then I went over to the desk and on a sheet of poster paper, I printed: THIS LIBRARY IS OPEN TO CHILDREN AND ADULTS DURING THE HOURS STATED BELOW. I walked outside and pasted it over the section of the sign which stated that children were only permitted to use the library on Tuesday and Thursday afternoons. It would have to suffice until a new sign could be commissioned. Then I went back inside and moved the wooden record stand over to the Adult Section.

If I had thought for one moment that being the town librarian would limit my involvement with marine life, I was sorely mistaken.

One morning while I was busy shelving books before opening, the telephone shrilled on the desk. It was the switchboard operator phoning from the municipal offices, one block away.

'Chrystal, we have a German couple here, with a dolphin they found on the beach.'

'A dolphin!'

'Yes. I'm sending them over to you, perhaps you can contact your husband.'

'But . . .' Too late, the connection was dead.

I knew that Dave and Johannes were out on farm calls that morning. What on earth was I going to do with a dolphin in the library? It couldn't have happened on a worse day, as I was expecting a visit from two senior provincial library officials later that morning. They were coming to meet me to discuss extensions to the library.

Deep in thought, I wandered through to the bathroom and stood gazing down at the old bathtub. It was quite big – but big enough for a dolphin? Just then, there was a muffled knock on the front door.

I opened it warily to find a middle-aged couple standing on the steps. Cradled in the man's arms was a very tired baby penguin.

'Oh, it's a penguin!' I exclaimed in relief.

'A pinkwin?' the man uttered, looking confused.

'Yes, it's a penguin, not a dolphin,' I explained. They did not appear to understand English. Gesturing to them to follow me, I grabbed a few old newspapers and walked

through to the bathroom. After lining the bath with newspaper, I removed the penguin from the man's arms and stood it in the bath.

Because of our communication problem, I was unable to explain about my husband being a vet or about taking the penguin home at lunchtime. The couple left, looking very troubled.

'Einer pinkwin?' I heard the woman say as they descended the steps.

'Ja, Ja, einer pinkwin,' her husband nodded.

'In einer bibliothek? Mit einem buch?'

'Ja, in einer badewanne,' he added pensively.

The two provincial officials arrived a few hours later. Mr Stephenson was a good-looking man in his late thirties, with the cultured air of an English gentleman, and Ms Redgrove was an attractive woman about the same age as myself. I made tea and we sat around the table discussing extensions to the existing building.

After tea, Mr Stephenson asked to use the toilet. Without giving it a second thought, I said, 'It's down the passage to the left,' and I carried on chatting to Ms Redgrove.

Five minutes later, Mr Stephenson rejoined us.

'Errm,' he said, clearing his throat.

We paused in our conversation to gaze up at him.

'There would appear to be a penguin in the bath,' he remarked and I noticed that his left eyebrow was positioned some two inches higher than his right.

'Yes?' I said.

'Do you always keep a penguin in the bath?'

'No. It's just for today. Just for the morning actually.'

'Ah,' he nodded. 'Just for the morning.'

The conversation seemed to grind to a halt and they left shortly afterwards.

Moving On

There is no easy way to tell you this.

Philby died. He died on the second last day of November, a day before we were due to vacate the sea-house again.

We had known for several weeks that there was something wrong. Something seriously wrong. It began with a slight loss of appetite and, as the days passed, he began to eat less and less. At first Dave suspected a flare-up of the feline leukaemia he'd diagnosed five years previously, shortly after we'd adopted Philby. At times Philby's temperature would soar and he'd become feverish and lethargic. The cytotoxic drugs we'd used to treat him when he was first diagnosed were no longer available. The human alternatives were far too strong for a cat, Dave was informed. He started him on a course of antibiotics but as the weeks went by there was no improvement.

'I think we may be dealing with more than feline leukaemia here,' Dave told me. 'His abdomen has a pulpy feel to it.'

'What does that mean?'

'I think he may have feline infectious peritonitis.'

My heart skipped a beat and I gazed at him in horror. My knowledge of the disease was limited to three facts. There was no prevention, no treatment and no cure.

'What can we do?'

'I'll have to perform an exploratory laparotomy to confirm my diagnosis. His condition is deteriorating and we can't let him go on like this.'

'When?'

'Tomorrow, then you can be with him.' The next day was a Saturday and the library was closed.

That night I lay in bed, cradling Philby in my arms. Normally he did not enjoy being cuddled. He was not that kind of cat. But this night was different. He lay peacefully in my arms, his body as light as a feather, despite his big frame. We didn't talk much. Mostly I prayed, prayed that it was something else.

It was feline infectious peritonitis. Dave injected the euthanase while Philby was still under anaesthetic. It broke my heart.

I woke early the next morning and lay in bed, gazing dully at the open windows. I wished that the day would just go away. Later, Dave rose and went to wake Johannes. He returned with the news that Johannes had been on a bender the night before and was in no state to help us move from the sea-house. I stared at him with swollen red eyes. It didn't matter. Nothing really mattered.

The previous year I had begun packing two weeks before the move. This year, because I was working, there hadn't been time. In the evenings I was too tired and the weekends seemed to flash by in a haze of good intentions.

Friends of Dodo and Bill had offered us the use of a cottage adjoining their house and we'd accepted gratefully. Dodo and Bill were not getting any younger and although they denied it, we knew that our annual descent upon them was disruptive.

'I'll pack the boxes and you can load them into the bakkie,' I told Dave, haphazardly flinging possessions into cardboard boxes.

Both the cottage and the house had been closed up for more than a year and when we arrived with the first load and opened the front door a smell of damp and dust rose up to greet us. We began sneezing violently.

'We'll have to clean the place before we can even think of unpacking,' I said to Dave and he sped back to the sea-house to fetch the vacuum cleaner.

I wandered outside into the beautiful old garden and sank down on to the cool earth beneath a huge mulberry tree. Dapples of sunlight glinted through the leafy branches, warming my face as tears streamed down my cheeks.

Late that afternoon we loaded the last boxes and while Dave settled the animals into the bakkie, I turned and walked back inside the sea-house. I checked each room to make sure that nothing had been left behind. I paused in the sitting room to gaze out through the windows at the sparkling sea. Then I turned and walked out on to the veranda, pulling the door shut behind me. I knew that we would not be coming back.

That evening Dave asked me where I wanted Philby buried. 'We still have a day before the holiday people move in. We could bury him under the tree aloe next to Splittie.'

'No.'

'Where then?'

'Here. Under the mulberry tree.'

A few days later we gave June one month's notice.

The following weekend my cousin Carmen came to visit. On the Saturday night we made a fire in the barbecue area next to the cottage. While we were sitting around the fire chatting, the telephone rang and Dave went to answer it. Five minutes later he returned, looking troubled.

'That was Mr Peters, Chief of Sea Rescue Services. A ship has capsized off the coast near Seal Bay,' he said.

Seal Bay was just west of Dolphin Bay.

'When?'

'A few hours ago, just after sunset. They managed to rescue the crew, but apparently the ship was carrying oil and while they were busy with the rescue they noticed quite a few penguins in trouble.'

'Oh no!'

'Unfortunately there was nothing they could do to help the penguins because of the fading light and heavy seas. Mr Peters wondered if we could assemble a group of volunteers and go out at first light?'

'We could ask Jenny.'

'Yes, that's what I thought. He mentioned that the road ends about two kilometres from the area, which forms part of a marine reserve. I told him that the bakkie is not a four-wheel drive but he says he'll transport us along the beach for the last two kilometres in his jeep.'

Dave went off to phone Jenny. By this time the fire had died down and we decided to skip supper and have an early night.

Just before dawn the next morning Jenny and her two

teenage sons arrived, followed shortly afterwards by several young men in two vans. We loaded their vehicles and our bakkie with the boxes we had used in the move and drove in convoy to Seal Bay, which was some forty-five minutes away by road.

Nic grumbled about being turfed out of his warm bed so early in the morning but Dodo and Bill were away and he had to come with us.

'I'll keep him occupied while you catch penguins,' Carmen offered. 'I've never done this kind of thing before.'

'Nor have we.'

Mr Peters was waiting for us in the front seat of a rusted old jeep parked on the grass verge in front of his house.

'Follow me,' he called out and we followed his jeep along winding dirt roads lined with thick bush. Eventually he pulled over at a spot where a sandy track led up over a sand dune and down on to the beach.

'This is as far as your vehicles can go,' he said. 'From here on we'll have to use the jeep.'

The jeep wasn't big enough to accommodate all of us plus the boxes so we decided to load the boxes into the rear canopied section. Carmen, Nic and I would ride in front with Mr Peters and once he had offloaded us and the boxes, he would return for the others. In the mean time they would start walking the two-kilometre stretch along the beach.

'From what we could see last night, the area most heavily affected is off a large plateau of rock which extends out into the sea, almost like a peninsula,' Mr Peters told us, as the jeep ploughed manfully across the soft sand.

'No beach at all, just rock?' I asked.

'No beach at all. It's going to be tricky retrieving penguins from the water. In places, there's a sheer drop into the sea.'

'Are there any sloping areas?'

'On one side the rocks do slope down gradually into the water but the other side consists of small sheer cliffs, a few metres high. Mind you, there are a few gullies,' he added.

I digested this information in silence, watching the huge breakers tumble on to the shore.

'The sea is quite rough today,' I observed.

'Yes, and it's even worse at the point.'

'I'll keep Nic away from the water,' Carmen offered.

'Thank you.'

The sand petered out ahead of us and the jeep veered on to a rocky potholed track for a short distance before coming to a halt.

'We'll have to offload here,' said Mr Peters.

As we climbed down from the jeep, I could smell the oil. Fumes seared my nostrils and my eyes began to water. Nic started rubbing his eyes and I wondered what it must be like to be submerged in it.

The jeep droned off back along the beach and I looked around curiously. We were on a large plateau of rock. Twenty metres ahead of us and to the left, clouds of white spray billowed above the plateau. To the right, waves churned up on to an uneven rocky shore and as I looked I spotted a penguin hunched miserably on a rock, and then another, and another.

'Look,' I said to Carmen, 'they're all over the place.'

'Do you want to start catching? I'll stay here with Nic.'

'No, I'll wait for the others. They're quite close to the water's edge and I don't want to frighten them back into the sea. We may have to try and cut them off somehow.'

Fifteen minutes later the jeep arrived with the rest of the group and as Dave clambered down, he sniffed the air.

'This doesn't smell like oil, it smells more like petrol.'

'The crew mentioned transformer oil,' said Mr Peters.

We decided to start with the area which sloped down into the sea and, forming a pincer movement, we approached the penguins from the sea side. Despite being oiled they were still strong and very fast. Some allowed themselves to be caught fairly easily, while others scrambled wildly over rocks and into pools in a desperate bid to escape.

Slipping and sliding on the rocks, I made my way towards a large adult who was crouched in the lee of a boulder. It watched my approach warily, its head swaying from side to side, like a snake covering all fronts. Squatting down, I extended my left hand, waggling it slightly. As it focused on my left hand, I shot out my right and gripped it behind the neck. With a honk of pure terror, it thrashed around violently and I struggled to maintain my grip on the oil-slippy feathers. Quick as lightning, before I knew what was happening, it closed its beak on the flesh of my left arm. My shrieks of pain mingled with its honks.

Eventually I managed to free myself and with one hand under its belly and the other clasping its neck, I stumbled back across the rocks to the jeep. As Carmen opened the canopy door, I lowered it into the box.

'How many do we have?'

'Five.'

Two hours and twenty-five penguins later, we had cleared the sloping area and we turned our attention to the other side. Dave and I approached the edge of one of the small cliffs and stared down at the sheer rock face which ended in the sea three metres below. From where we stood we could see large patches of iridescent oil drifting uneasily on the heaving surface.

'Dave, this is going to be impossible.' I shook my head doubtfully.

'And extremely dangerous,' Dave observed.

We spotted a few penguins wallowing in gullies between the cliffs, being tossed to and fro as waves surged in and sucked back. We called the others and, forming a human chain, we managed to pluck one penguin from the water.

One and a half hours later, we had only managed to rescue another five and we decided to call it a day. It was just too risky.

'Hopefully those that are left will make their way on to the rocky slope,' said Mr Peters. 'I'll try and get a team out here tomorrow.'

On the way back to Dolphin Bay we discussed the situation. The cages at the surgery were all occupied by sick animals and there were no facilities for keeping a large group of penguins at the cottage. Dave felt that this time we needed help.

When we arrived back at the surgery he telephoned the Oceanarium in Port Elizabeth. They offered to take the penguins and we decided to transport them there immediately and tube them on arrival, rather than offloading them and then having to load them again.

Over the next few days, individual penguins were brought in, in dribs and drabs, and Dave treated and hospitalised them at the surgery. In the mean time, we heard that the staff and volunteers at the Oceanarium were battling to cope with the larger group, as the toxic effects of the transformer oil became apparent and birds began to die. A decision was taken to fly the penguins to SANCCOB, the penguin rehabilitation centre in Cape Town, for specialist attention.

A few days later newspaper headlines announced that many were dead on arrival, while others died shortly afterwards. The transformer oil had burned their eyes, mouths, intestines and lungs and in the end the mortality rate was around eighty per cent. We managed to save a few of those brought to the surgery but, all in all, there was no happy ending.

Two months later, we moved into a cottage just down the road from the surgery. It was small but it was permanent. Now that both of us were working, moving out once a year in December promised to become a nightmare.

But it wasn't only that.

I knew that for a long time the sea-house would be alive with memories of Philby. He would be in every corner of every room and in every nook and cranny of the garden and in the dunes and in the sound of the sea at night. It would hurt too much.

The Doppelgänger

'Dave, come quickly! She has a gun!' I called urgently, rushing into the garden.

'Who? Who has a gun?'

'Bernadette. She says she's going to kill her husband.'

'WHAT!'

It had all started quite innocently with a phone call from one of Dave's colleagues in the neighbouring town of Cougadorp. Someone had left an oiled penguin on the doorstep of his clinic and as he had not dealt with penguins before, he wanted to send it to us.

'That's fine,' Dave told him. 'How will you get it to us?'

'Well, that's the problem. I'm too busy to bring it myself and I wondered if you knew of anyone who could pick it up?'

'I'll see what I can do,' Dave promised. He recalled hearing that the husband of one of our clients ran a business in Cougadorp and travelled back and forth each day. When Dave contacted Bernadette, she said they would love to help.

'I'll phone Marcos immediately,' she told Dave. 'It's

almost closing time, so he should have the penguin at the surgery by 5.30.'

'Ask him to drop it off at the cottage,' Dave said. 'We're closing a bit earlier.' He sent Johannes over to me with the message that a penguin was on its way.

At 5.30 the telephone rang in the cottage and when I answered, a voice asked abruptly: 'Has Marcos arrived?'

'Oh, hello Bernadette. No, he hasn't arrived yet.'

'What is taking him so long? He should've been there already.'

'Don't worry, I'm sure he's on his way.' I was still speaking when she slammed the phone down.

Bernadette was of Spanish extraction. She was an excellent animal owner, albeit a bit excitable.

When Dave arrived home I mentioned her call.

'She seemed a bit upset.'

'I think that their marriage might be going through a rough patch,' he said.

'Oh.'

Dave wandered out to the back garden with Nic and the dogs. Shrieks of delight wafted into the house as Nic tossed a ball for Whippy.

'BRING Whippy . . . BRING!' he shrilled.

Just after six o'clock the phone rang again and this time I lifted the receiver warily.

'Is he there yet?' Bernadette asked angrily.

'No, not yet. But I'm sure he'll be here any minute now.'

'THE BASTARD!' she yelled, slamming the phone down in my ear yet again. I stood for a moment, staring at the receiver in my hand. Dave was right. There was definitely a problem here, I thought uneasily.

Twenty minutes later someone hammered loudly on the front door and I trotted down the passage and into the sitting

The Doppelgänger

room. When I opened the door it was to find Bernadette pacing the veranda.

'Where is he?' she demanded.

'Who?' I asked stupidly, wondering if she wanted to see Dave.

'MARCOSSS,' she spat out the word, glaring at me.

'We're still waiting for him.'

Slightly at a loss, I stood in the doorway as she paced up and down, hissing foreign words under her breath. Just then we heard a vehicle screech to a halt in the road outside. Bernadette swung round and stared. 'HA,' she snorted triumphantly, 'now I'm going to KILL the swine.' Whipping up her T-shirt, she pulled out a revolver from a holster strapped to her hip.

'Bernadette . . . don't,' I began weakly, but she ignored me and rocketed down the steps towards the driveway, waving the revolver in the air.

In the back garden, Dave stared at me in disbelief.

'Dave, I think we should call the police.'

'Chrystal, are you sure it's a gun? Maybe it's a bleeper or something?'

'It's a GUN, I tell you! Do something!'

He sighed. 'OK, take Nic and the animals inside and I'll go and see what's happening.'

With a dismissive look Mandy loped off after Dave, ignoring my order to 'come'. I knew what she was thinking. If people with guns were lurking outside, she was not about to be closed in with the women and children.

Entering our bedroom, I moved over to the window and peered out cautiously. My blood ran cold at the sight which met my eyes. Bernadette was standing in the middle of the road facing Dave, her gun pointing directly at his chest. Dave had hold of Mandy's collar to prevent her from leaping for Bernadette's throat, something she was obviously dying to do. Marcos was huddled behind Dave, helplessly clutching a cardboard box. And from the open top of the box, a penguin peeped out nervously.

'*It's a Boeing 747,*' Carrots whispered at my side.

'What?'

'*The gun, it's a Boeing 747.*'

'But that's an aeroplane!'

'*No, it's a type of gun . . . Philby told me, he taught me all about guns.*'

I stared at him, momentarily distracted from the scene outside. Then Bernadette shouted: 'MOVE ASIDE . . . LET ME SHOOT THE BASTARD AND GET IT OVER WITH!'

'Get down on the floor,' I ordered Nic. 'Stay down and don't move. I have to help Dad.'

I raced down the passage and out on to the lawn. Glancing back at the window, I spotted Nic, Whippy and Carrots peeping out, only their eyes and the tops of their heads visible above the sill.

'GET DOWN . . . AND STAY DOWN!' I yelled and they sank from sight.

'Move aside!' Bernadette shrieked. 'Move aside, or you will get hurt.'

As she tried to edge around Dave, he moved to block her. Glancing at me, he said quietly, 'Chrystal, get the penguin.' Marcos nodded gratefully as I took the box from his hands and ran back to the veranda where I deposited it in a corner. As I raced back to the group, I heard Dave say, 'Bernadette, hand me the gun . . . just hand me the gun.'

'Yes,' I said desperately. 'Give him the gun and let's all go inside and have a nice cup of tea and a valium.'

The look she gave me made my toes curl but while her attention was diverted, Marcos dived out from behind Dave and grabbed her gun arm. Dave let go of Mandy's collar and sprang to his assistance. As they lurched around the road grappling for possession of the gun, there was a deafening 'CRACK' and a bullet whizzed off in the direction of the surgery. My eyes followed its trajectory and I glimpsed two people dive for cover behind a parked car.

Somehow, in the aftershock of the explosion, Marcos managed to wrest the gun from Bernadette's grasp and raced to his car and jumped in. Mandy leapt forward as Bernadette launched herself after Marcos. Bernadette collided with Mandy's body, stumbled and almost fell. Marcos screeched off down the road, wheels spinning.

'YOU BASTARD, I'LL GET YOU!' Bernadette shouted as she flung herself into her car and roared off after him. At that precise moment a police van screamed down the road towards us. As it drew level, we pointed to the two vehicles careering off into the distance and the van sped off after them. We watched all three vehicles disappear around a corner. After a few moments, in absolute silence, we walked across the grass towards the veranda.

Nic and Whippy and Carrots were leaning from the bedroom window, their eyes the size of golf balls.

'Mom, Mom, why was that lady trying to shoot that man?' Nic called out excitedly.

'I think she was cross with him,' I called back.

At my side, Dave murmured something about a penguin.

'Pardon?'

'I said, thank God we managed to save the penguin.'

'Oh. Yes.'

Prior to our moving into the cottage, Jenny had lived there for a year, after selling her house which was just down the road on the opposite side.

When she first put her house on the market, Dave and I had discussed buying it. But by no stretch of the imagination or our finances could we afford it and after a few weeks it was sold to a young dentist.

On our very first visit to Jenny's house, which she had named 'The Greenhouse', we had fallen in love with it. The house was quite old and nestled amongst gracious old trees on a double plot. In the front garden a huge lemon tree sent its fragrance out into the road and the walls were draped in vivid flowering creepers. In the back garden a round aquamarine swimming pool was set in a brick patio just outside the glass sliding doors of the sitting room, creating an atmosphere of cool green restfulness.

When we moved into the cottage we'd pass The Greenhouse on our way to and from the surgery each day and often I'd gaze at it wistfully and wish it was ours.

Mrs Kowalski, a Polish émigré who represented the owners of the cottage, lived just down the road and around the corner. When Jenny's new house on the beach was built she approached Mrs Kowalski about our taking over the lease of the cottage and Mrs Kowalski agreed.

The cottage was tiny. If two people were busy in the kitchen, then it was one person too many. Most of the floor space in our bedroom, which overlooked the street, was taken up by our double-bed. Nic's bedroom consisted of an alcove off the passageway to the sitting room and at night when he was asleep, we'd tiptoe quietly past his bed on our way from the sitting room to our bedroom. A garage adjoined the cottage and initially we converted this into a bedroom for Johannes, until we could find more suitable accommodation for him.

We missed the spacious airiness of the sea-house and its close proximity to the sea. But the cottage was only two blocks from the beach and once we'd settled in, the dogs and I began jogging again. Sometimes Carrots and Nuggie would tag along and, occasionally, Seafood. Fluffy had decided that she was too old for jaunts on the beach. She said the soft sand made her joints creak.

When the first faint light sifted into the sky, we'd cross the road and amble down the wide grass verge past three houses to the main road. Here I'd stop to pick up the cats, carrying them over the main road to the steps leading down on to the beach. The early morning sand would be silky-cool on the surface and warm underneath. As the dogs and I set off on our run, the cats would drift off to explore the dunes near the steps.

In my mind, this hour before dawn became *dolphin hour*. Almost every morning we'd see streams of them hunting just offshore, the water thick with their bodies gleaming purple-blue in the early light. They'd glide in and out of the waves with fluid ease, only a few metres away from us as we ran. Often the dogs would sense their presence long before I spotted them. Ears pricked, they'd gaze out to sea with an introspective look, as if plugging into a conversation that I was not privy to.

One morning as I sprinted along the waterline, feet splashing in the shallows, Mandy and Arrow, who were racing ahead, stopped abruptly to stare into a pool formed by a channel between two shelves of rocks. Coming up behind them, I saw what appeared to be the small drenched face of a dog gazing up at me.

'Come away,' I called to the dogs. 'It's scared of you.' Mandy, Arrow and Flenny moved up on to the dry sand but, with an obstinate look, Whippy remained at my side and we approached the pool together.

The light-brown dog was treading water, only its eyes and small rounded ears visible above the surface.

'It's all right,' I murmured encouragingly. 'You can come out now. They won't hurt you.'

It stared back at us, not moving. Afraid that it would be sucked out to sea, I walked into the waist-deep water holding out my hand. I waded slowly forwards but when I was one metre away, with a sudden swirl of water it turned and glided swiftly beyond the rocks. And as it turned, I saw the long bushy tail.

'Good heavens, it's an otter!' I uttered in amazement.

The otter paused just beyond the rocks, floating gently on the currents and looking at me with interest. I gazed back, equally curious. After a while it seemed to become bored and, turning once more, it slid out into the waves. As I watched, it surfed a huge wave, its body clearly visible against the silvery-green water.

'Look at me,' it seemed to be saying gleefully. *'See what I can do!'*

Thoughts of preparing breakfast and getting ready for work evaporated like sea mist before the sun. I lost track of time and watched, enchanted, as its body sliced through one wave after another, one minute a rigid surfboard, the next a sinuous acrobat. Every now and then I giggled aloud at its antics. This otter was showing off!

Gradually the waves carried it further and further down the bay away from us and finally I stirred. 'Come on,' I said to the dogs. 'We must get back.'

As we ran back towards the steps, I reflected on the

encounter. Somehow I felt privileged. As if a great honour had been bestowed upon me.

'How can I concentrate on my poetry, with Rambo jumping on me all the time?' Nuggie moaned as he stumbled into the kitchen, the fur on the top of his head all awry.

'Who's Rambo?'

'Carrots. I don't know what's got into him. He swaggers around, armed to the teeth and then he jumps on me and says he's practising his Kung-fu.'

'Kung-fu!'

'Yes. Poets cannot work with this type of activity going on. They need peace and quiet.'

'I'm sorry.'

'So am I. I had just composed a particularly brilliant line of "To a mouse" and now I can't remember it.'

'It's been done before.'

'What?'

' "To a mouse." It's been done before.'

'Are you sure?'

'Yes.'

'Oh.'

'You could write one about a rat.'

'I suppose so. But you must speak to Carrots.'

'I will, I promise.'

Nuggie wandered off. Deep in thought, I carried on slicing bread. Carrots had been acting strangely ever since Philby died. Only a few days before, he had attacked a Great Dane on the beach.

We were descending the steps on to the sand when a gunmetal-grey dog, the size of a small donkey, bounded up to us, tail wagging, tongue lolling from its mouth. Whippy, Mandy, Arrow and Flenny were introducing themselves when suddenly a whirlwind of feline fury erupted from the dunes.

Carrots, his ginger fur bushed-up and sparking as if electrified, flew at the unfortunate animal with all the intent of Genghis Khan on a good day. As his claws raked the dog's buttocks, it gave one terrified yowl and, leaping into the air with its tail between its legs, it turned to run. With Carrots in hot determined pursuit.

'CARROTS!' I screamed. 'STOP . . . YOU'RE GOING TO GET BITTEN!'

With one final burst of desperate speed the dog shot off down the beach. Springing forward, I grabbed Carrots by the tail and scooped him up into my arms.

'Are you MAD?' I hissed. 'You cannot attack Great Danes just like that. Look at the SIZE of the animal!'

With a satisfied smirk, Carrots lay back in my arms, purring contentedly.

I wrapped the last sandwich in foil and went to look for Carrots. He was on the couch in the sitting room, watching TV.

'What are you watching?' I asked, sitting down next to him.

'Reservoir cats.'
'Oh. Carrots?'
'Yes?'
'What's the matter?'
'What do you mean?'
'You've been behaving so strangely, more like a Philby

than a Carrots.'

'*Oh.*' He looked embarrassed.

'Do you want to tell me why?'

'*Well,*' he said, shifting uneasily on the couch, '*it's just . . .*'

'Yes?'

'*It's just that I know you miss Philby.*'

'Yes?'

'*And I thought . . . if I was more like him, then you wouldn't miss him so much.*'

'Ah,' I nodded. 'I see.'

'*Am I being silly?*'

'A bit. You see, if you become Philby, then I'd lose Carrots.'

'*Oh! I never thought of it like that. Would you mind?*'

'What?'

'*Losing Carrots.*'

'Very much.'

'*I think I'll have to stop being Philby then,*' he said. And he looked very relieved.

'I think so. Would you like a little snack?'

'*Yes, please.*'

'Let's go and see what we can find.'

At a Push

From the start, Silverkitty didn't like the cottage and one day, a few weeks after we moved in, he disappeared. Late the following afternoon on my way home from the library, I stopped in at the sea-house. As I drove down the long driveway I could see at a glance that the house was still unoccupied, the windows tightly shut, the curtains drawn. The plants in the corner of the veranda were dead and shrivelled.

Calling, 'Silverkitty ... Silverkitty,' I strolled down the side of the house to the front garden.

He was sitting on the old wooden table in the middle of the lawn. Waiting for me.

'You silly cat, we don't live here any longer,' I smiled, perching on the table next to him. As I gazed out over the sea, he rubbed up against me, purring happily. Tranquil evening waves painted in sunset pink-and-gold whispered on to the shore and I spotted Ruth on the rocks, her dog at her side. Just beyond the last wave a smooth dark hulk of rock crouched amidst the gleaming waters. We'd named it 'Black Rock'. At high tide it was totally submerged.

Filled with a sudden longing, I sat quietly, half-expecting Philby to hop up next to me or to glimpse Splittie stomping past on her way to the beach. After a while I rose and picked Silverkitty up in my arms and carried him to the bakkie.

He remained at the cottage for a week before disappearing again. I fetched him from the sea-house on my way home from work, but he did it again and again.

Then one afternoon he wasn't there and the only response to my calls was the plaintive cries of seagulls overhead.

'Some cats become more attached to a place than to people,' Dave told me. I accepted this but, even so, I continued to stop in at the sea-house every few days. One afternoon as I turned into the driveway, I found a dark-green Combi blocking my path. I mounted the steps on to the veranda and knocked on the open door and a young man appeared. I explained about Silverkitty and he promised to contact us should Silverkitty turn up. He and three friends were sharing the house, he told me.

We never heard from them. Silverkitty's departure mimicked his arrival. Despite enquiries, we had never been able to establish his origins. He had simply appeared from thin air. And now he was gone ... back into thin air. A quantum cat.

I worried about him. Was he getting enough to eat?

'He'll cope,' Dave reassured me. 'He's a survivor.'

'If only I knew he was safe.'

'Chrystal, it was his decision to leave.'

'Yes, I know, but ...'

We didn't know it at the time, but we were to see him again ... several years later.

'Excuse me, are you the vet?'

Busy with record cards, Dave glanced up to see two

young men standing at the counter; one was dark-haired and the other was blond.

'Yes.'

'We need some information,' said the dark-haired one.

'Yes?'

'What do penguins eat?'

'They eat fish. Why?'

'Tinned fish or fresh fish?'

'Fresh fish. They're not likely to find tinned fish in the sea.'

'What kind of fresh fish?'

'Mostly pilchards. Look, why are you asking me this? Have you found a penguin?'

'No reason,' the young man said evasively. 'We're on holiday here and we just wondered. Thanks for your time.'

They turned to leave and, on an impulse, Dave rose and followed them out of the waiting room to their car which was parked in the road just outside. Seated in the front passenger seat was a young woman, a closed cardboard box on her lap.

'What do you have in there?' Dave asked casually, coming up behind them. They jumped guiltily and after a moment's hesitation, the fair-haired young man blurted out, 'Actually we do have a penguin. We found it on the beach.'

'I see. What are you planning to do with it?'

'Well it seems very tame and we thought we'd take it back to Johannesburg with us. We have a swimming-pool at home,' he explained.

'Do you want it to die?' Dave asked.

'NO . . . NO!' they chorused, looking shocked.

'Dealing with any wild species requires a certain degree of knowledge and specialised facilities,' Dave pointed out. 'If you have neither, you would be taking it to a certain death.'

'I told you it was a silly idea,' the young woman piped up.

'Anyway, let's have a look,' Dave said calmly and the young woman opened the box.

Lying inside, in an obvious state of collapse, was a very small baby penguin. Dave reached in and lifted it from the box.

'It's very young,' he said. 'And it's not tame, it's extremely weak.'

The three trailed after him into the consulting room and watched in embarrassed silence as Dave examined the little penguin.

'It's very dehydrated. If you had fed it fish you would have killed it,' he told them. 'When they're dehydrated like this, they cannot digest fish properly.'

'We're sorry, we didn't intend any harm.'

'Besides being dehydrated,' Dave continued, 'it also has fluid in the lungs.'

They stared at him.

'And what's more,' Dave said sternly, 'anyone caught transporting a penguin from its natural habitat would face a hefty fine and a possible jail sentence.'

The three appeared totally unnerved by this piece of information and they left shortly afterwards.

Dave tubed the penguin with electrolyte solution and injected an antibiotic for the lung problem. It hovered between life and death for three days. On the fourth day it managed to stand, although rather unsteadily and we began feeding it tiny slivers of fish. Dave decided to name it 'Lucky'.

'What about *Very Lucky*,' I suggested, remembering Johannesburg.

There was a small duck pond in the back garden of the cottage. We erected a makeshift wooden shelter next to it and enclosed the area with wire. One Sunday morning, when Lucky had been taking whole fish for a few days, we moved him to the enclosure. We would have to keep him there until he was ready for release.

Dodo and Bill had invited us to lunch at a local hotel that day, in celebration of a wedding anniversary. After a three-course meal and several glasses of champagne, we drove home feeling distinctly replete.

'I'm going to take a nap,' I told Dave.

'Me too,' he said, yawning widely.

Nic was fast asleep on my lap and he didn't stir as we carried him from the bakkie to his bed.

Before we lay down we went to check on Lucky and found him gambolling happily in the duck pond. Ten minutes later, just as we were drifting off to sleep, the dogs jumped up and began barking furiously at the front door. 'Oh no!' I moaned. 'Not now!'

Dave rose reluctantly and stumbled through to the sitting room. I heard voices in the distance and was just dozing off again when he walked into the room carrying a cardboard box.

'What's in the box?' I asked sleepily.

'A cat . . . and three kittens.'

'Whose cat is it?'

'Ours, I think.'

I sat up in bed. 'Where did they come from?'

'I'll tell you later. I need to find a place for them. They can't stay in the box and I don't feel like going over to the surgery now.'

'We can make a bed for them in the bathroom,' I suggested. 'You can take them to the surgery this evening.'

Dave carried the box through to the bathroom and placed it on the floor. I closed the window and crouched down next to the box. Suddenly I thought of Splittie and, with a sense of déjà vu, I lifted the flaps. As I lifted the last flap, two very alert light-green eyes, set in a grey and white triangular face, looked at me warily. She was long-haired, her coat a kaleidoscope of grey, white and orange splashes.

'Hello,' I said. 'What's your name?'

'It's "Puss",' Dave said, entering the bathroom with a cushion and a thick blanket.

I stared at him. 'Is that in English or Afrikaans?' (The pronunciation of the two is identical, but while the English word is an affectionate term for a cat, the Afrikaans version, like the American, is a rather crude word.)

'Afrikaans, I would imagine,' Dave said with a cynical look. 'If their laughter was anything to go by.'

When Dave had opened the front door, there was no one there, only a small cardboard box squatting on the veranda. As he stepped over the box, he spotted a tall young man striding down the driveway.

'Excuse me,' Dave called out.

The young man turned. 'Hello Doc,' he said cheerfully. 'I've brought you a cat and three kittens.'

'I don't want a cat and three kittens,' Dave said irritably.

'I'm off to sea for three months,' the young man explained. 'There's no one to look after them.'

'Why don't you ask one of your friends?'

'They're not into cats.'

'Well, what do you expect me to do with them?'

'Do what you like. You're the vet.'

'Exactly! I'm a vet, not a dumping ground for irresponsible pet-owners. And look at this box! It's far too small to hold a cat and three kittens and there are no air holes.'

The young man shrugged carelessly. 'Sorry Doc, have to rush,' he said, turning towards a large truck parked in the road. Several disreputable-looking characters were lolling from the open back of the truck. The young man swung himself up into the cab and as the truck pulled away, he shouted, 'THE CAT'S NAME IS PUSS.' At this, the disreputable-looking characters broke into raucous laughter.

'Ha hah harrr,' they roared. 'HA HAH HARRR,' and Dave looked on helplessly as the truck disappeared down the road.

'We can't call her that!' I exclaimed.

'No, we'll have to find another name for her.'

'Look at her kittens, Dave. They're beautiful.'

As we gazed down at the three bundles of fluff, Whippy sneaked her head around the door.

With an ear-splitting yowl, the mother-cat rose in the air as if levitating and flew at Whippy. Dave sprang to stop her, but as he gripped her behind the neck, she lashed out at Whippy's face. With a shriek of pain, Whippy tumbled backwards and I leapt up to shut the door.

Leaving Dave to calm the mother-cat, I rushed off to find Whippy. She was huddled behind our bedroom door, looking upset. Blood was streaming from the slash on her cheek.

'What are you doing behind the door?'

'Hiding.'

'You can come out now, she's closed in the bathroom and I need to disinfect that cut.'

'Why did she attack me like that? I just wanted to see the kittens.'

'I know. But it was a bit silly of you, her being a strange cat.'

'But that's the only time I get to see kittens,' Whippy moaned. *'None of our cats ever has kittens,'* she added resentfully.

'They're all spayed. Anyway, you had puppies of your own once.'

'I would've preferred kittens.'

'Yes, well . . . that's not how it works.'

That evening Dave took the mother-cat and her kittens to the surgery. Not wanting to cage her, he made a bed for them in the small storeroom situated in an alcove off the consulting room.

'She settled down immediately,' he said. 'I think she'll be fine there.'

And she was.

Until the first consultation the next morning.

As Dave ushered Mr Kapp and his bulldog Charles into the consulting room, he heard a faint rustle coming from the direction of the storeroom. He turned towards the sound and was confronted by the sight of the mother-cat, claws unfurled like razors as she charged straight at Charles. With one shocked look, his eyes bulging in terror, Charles bolted under the consulting table, dragging Mr Kapp after him.

'Johannes and I had a time of it, catching her,' Dave said ruefully. 'By the time we managed to get her into a cage, Mr Kapp and Charles were firmly wedged under the table. Charles' lead was entangled around its legs and we had to lift the table to free them.'

'What did Mr Kapp say?'

'He was very nice about it really. He said he'd come back another day. When Charles was feeling better.'

Unfortunately, during the fracas, Dave had been forced to shout, 'PUSS . . . PUSS!' at the top of his voice. He said Mr Kapp (who happened to be Afrikaans) had appeared reluctant to make eye-contact afterwards. We decided to change the mother-cat's name to 'Pushcat'.

We found homes for the three kittens a week later. It wasn't difficult, they were very attractive kittens. Once they had gone to their new homes, Pushcat calmed down and two weeks later, she moved into the cottage.

'I don't like the way she looks at me,' Whippy complained. *'She makes me nervous.'*

'She'll be fine now that the kittens have gone.'

'Where did they go?'

'To good homes.'

'We're a good home. Couldn't we have kept just one?'

'Then she'd still be attacking you.'

'If you say so,' Whippy uttered moodily.

Shortly after Pushcat moved in, Tony, the young dentist who had bought The Greenhouse, acquired a dog.

It was a cross between a Rottweiler and a German Shepherd, he informed Dave, when he brought it in for vaccination.

Bruno was already six months old and almost fully grown. His black and tan coat was short and thick. He had the broad head of a Rottweiler and the body of a German Shepherd, sturdy and powerful.

Tony was away at his practice during the day and, being single, he was out most evenings. After a few weeks we noticed that Bruno seemed lonely. He spent his days lying on the grass verge outside The Greenhouse and whenever we passed, he would leap up and bark at us aggressively. If the dogs were with us when this happened, Mandy would shoot him a filthy look, as if he was beneath contempt. Arrow and Flenny would simply gaze at him blankly, while poor old Whippy would glue herself to my leg. She had never been able to understand aggressive behaviour in humans or other animals. It was beyond her perception of things and she didn't know how to handle it. She just wanted everyone to be friends.

'Why can't we just be friends?' she asked me, after one such incident.

'It takes two to be friends.'

One evening, as I strolled by The Greenhouse with Nic just behind me on his scooter, Bruno sprang up and charged at Nic, barking ferociously and trying to bite the scooter wheels.

'BRUNO!' I shouted, running to intervene. 'STOP!' Turning from Nic, he snarled at me and I grabbed Nic by the hand and hurried away.

'That dog is becoming very aggressive,' I said to Dave when we got home.

'Which dog?'

'Bruno.'

'Hmmm, I've noticed. I think he's bored.'

'I'm worried about Nic. Bruno really went for him tonight.'

'Shall I have a word with Tony?'

'I don't think it will help. He's never home.'

'What do you suggest?'

'I think we must befriend him.'

And befriend him we did. Initially he regarded our overtures with deep suspicion. He would stare at us with cold blank eyes, a typical Rottweiler look, daring us to come closer.

'Just try and touch me,' that look said. *'Just try.'*

We didn't, but in passing, we'd speak to him.

'Hello Bruno,' we'd say. 'How are you today? Have you been a good boy?'

After a couple of weeks, we noticed that he was becoming less aggressive. He stopped barking at us and appeared almost puzzled by our overtures.

Late one afternoon, on my way down the road to the surgery, I saw Bruno sprawled on the pavement as usual and I called out, 'Hello, my boy.' He lifted his head and stared

at me. I noticed that the expression in his eyes seemed different and I paused for a moment to gaze at him thoughtfully.

Nic was waiting for me at the surgery and, carrying his packets of toys, we set off back down the road. As we drew level with The Greenhouse, Bruno saw us. He leapt up and bounded towards us.

'MOM!' Nic squealed in panic.

'It's OK, it's OK,' I said reassuringly. 'Look at his tail.'

That tail was wagging!

Bruno launched himself into the air and two huge front paws descended on my chest. I staggered back under the impact, dropping the packets of toys. As he slavered enthusiastically all over the front of my dress, I hugged him to me.

'See,' I said to Nic, 'he's trying to make friends.' Nic stiffened as Bruno turned his attention to him. 'Hold out your hand to him. Let him sniff it.' Nic extended his hand cautiously and immediately a large pink tongue flopped out and slobbered all over his fingers.

'Yeugh!' Nic protested, looking very relieved.

Before very long Bruno took to following us home, despite my efforts to prevent this.

'STAY,' I'd command sternly, gesturing towards The Greenhouse. He'd sink down on the pavement looking crestfallen, waiting only until my back was turned to spring up and lope after me.

'I think Bruno wants to come and live with us.'

'Well, he can't . . . he doesn't belong to us.'

'I know that.'

Changing Pace

Plans for extending the library were on track and a week before building operations were due to begin, at a meeting of the town clerk, provincial librarian and myself, it was decided that the library would have to close while building was in progress. The books would be removed from the shelves and stored elsewhere, as several internal walls were to be demolished. The builder and his team planned to start the following Monday and the Library Committee members volunteered to help me pack the books at the weekend.

On the Wednesday morning prior to this, I woke up feeling very nauseous. I struggled through the morning at the library and finally, just before lunchtime, I went to see my doctor.

'It's probably flu,' Dr Long said. 'There's a lot of it around at the moment. I think you should take the rest of the day off,' he added kindly. 'And tomorrow as well. Let's see how you are on Friday.'

I spent Thursday in bed. On the Friday morning, feeling worse than ever, I rose reluctantly and dragged myself through to the bathroom. As I brushed my teeth I glanced in the mirror and noticed that my eyes were yellow.

'My eyes are yellow,' I told Dave.

'No they're not, they're grey.'

'Not the irises, the whites. They're yellow.'

'Let's have a look.' He gazed into my eyes. 'I think you should see Dr Long.'

'Hepatitis,' pronounced Dr Long. 'The early symptoms resemble those of flu. I'll have to draw blood to confirm, but I want you to go home to bed and stay there.'

'But what about packing the books?' I protested.

'Someone else will have to do it. Hepatitis is not something you play around with. You may have to be confined to bed for six weeks.'

'SIX WEEKS!'

'If it's Type B, you'll have to have total rest for six weeks and avoid contact with other people. It's very contagious.'

'What about Nic and Dave?'

'You'll have to limit physical contact with them and keep your eating and drinking utensils separate. Look, I'll pop round tomorrow when the results of the blood tests are in. Then we'll know exactly what we're dealing with.'

I left his rooms and made my way to the municipal complex. In Mr Haig's office I positioned myself as far away as possible from him and explained about the hepatitis. And how contagious it could be. Hastily clasping a handkerchief to his mouth, he urged me to go home immediately.

'I'll get the Library Committee to pack the books,' he said, waving me away with his free hand.

Six weeks of pure misery followed. I ran fevers and my skin turned yellow.

'Now you're the same colour as Nuggie and me,' Carrots pointed out happily. He wasn't far off the mark I thought, staring at my face in the mirror. It glowed back at me like a sickly banana.

Because he was worried about the intensity of my

symptoms, Dr Long drew blood every few days in an attempt to identify the virus.

'It's Non-A, Non-B,' he informed me eventually, after several blood tests failed to produce a positive result for either Type A or Type B.

'Why do tests always show what I haven't got?'

'Non-A, Non-B is a type of viral hepatitis.'

'Why don't they just call it "C"?'

'You get Type C as well. Yours happens to be Non-A, Non-B.'

As the jaundiced blood cells began breaking down, I started itching. Whippy asked me if I had fleas.

After several weeks the nausea eased, but as my colour gradually returned to normal, my joints became increasingly stiff and sore. When I consulted Dr Long, he prescribed a course of anti-inflammatories and finally, after six long weeks at home, I returned to work.

The shelves at the library extended right down to the floor and despite the anti-inflammatories, I found it difficult to shelve books on the lower shelves. When I did bend it took some effort to straighten. I solved this by kneeling on the floor and crawling from one shelf to the next. Fortunately shelving of books was done when the library was closed to the public.

The hepatitis had left me feeling very debilitated and over the next three months I battled with colds and flu and, finally, pleurisy.

'We may be dealing with a flare-up of lupus,' Dr Long said. 'I think I should refer you to a specialist.'

'Let's wait a bit, maybe it'll pass.' I knew that a specialist meant tests. The two were synonymous.

Dr Long was going away for two weeks and he said we'd reassess the situation on his return.

A few days later my body seized up. It just simply seized up. Every joint became stiff and inflamed, feet, knees, hips, fingers, even my jaw. Overnight, walking became an exercise in agony. I made an appointment to see one of Dr Long's associates in Cougadorp and Bill offered to drive me there.

Bent almost double, unable to straighten my body, I lowered myself painfully into the chair opposite Dr Fourie.

'What's happened to you?' he asked curiously.

'I don't know,' I said, bursting into tears.

After examining me, he decided to admit me to hospital for six-hourly anti-inflammatory injections. 'We must get the inflammation under control,' he said. 'And I'm going to draw blood for some tests.' Bill drove me home where I packed a few things, and when I was ready Dave drove me back to the hospital.

The following morning Dr Fourie popped in to see me with the news that my anti-nuclear factor was sky-high. The lupus was on a roll.

'How are you feeling?'

'Better than yesterday.'

The injections seemed to be doing the trick. At least I could walk upright. If only the injection sites weren't so sore.

The first injection was given just after I was admitted. Dave was still with me when a short stocky sister with thick muscular arms strode into the ward.

'I need to give you an anti-inflammatory injection,' she stated brusquely. 'Will you roll over on to your side and expose your hip, please?' No sooner had I done so, than she flung the needle into my hip, like a missile. I yelped loudly as it struck home and she gave me a dirty look.

Six hours later, the next injection arrived in the hands of a very young nurse. The combined effect of her long vacant face and the cap resting on her eyebrows reminded me of a sheep.

'It's time for your next injection,' she mumbled uneasily, shifting from one foot to the other. 'Sister's busy and she's asked me to give it.'

I hoisted my nightgown up and watched apprehensively as she studied my hip in silence. Then she reached out a forefinger and began prodding it.

'What are you doing?' I asked in alarm.

'Looking for a fleshy spot. I don't want to stick it into bone.'

'No,' I agreed hastily. 'Please, take your time. Have you given many injections?'

'Hundreds,' she nodded and as I began to relax she added, 'to oranges.'

'Pardon?'

'Oranges. I'm a student nurse. We practise on oranges.'

As I curled up pretending to be an orange, she began rubbing a small area on my hip. Rub, rub, rub.

'If you rub long enough then the feeling goes,' she informed me stoically. Hoping she was right, I endured the rubbing in silence. Finally, when my nerves were strung as taut as piano wire, she reached into a pocket and produced the syringe.

'Are you ready?' she asked.

'Yesss,' I quavered.

With slow deliberate movements she manoeuvred the needle against my skin, piercing it carefully before pushing into the flesh. The pain was long and drawn out and I fought the temptation to shriek, 'HURRY UP!' After what seemed an eternity, she inched the needle out and I exhaled slowly.

Do oranges scream, I wondered?

After three days in hospital I was discharged, with hips resembling two lurid purple-blue sunsets.

While I had been in hospital, several oiled penguins had been brought in, Dave informed me.

'Some ship must have been cleaning its tanks at sea,' he said.

'I wish they wouldn't.'

'I know. Anyway, I've ordered several boxes of fish from a wholesaler. It's too expensive to keep buying fish in small quantities from the local shops.'

'But Dave, where will we store it?'

Storing the fish had always been a problem as the only freezing space we had was a small compartment in the surgery fridge.

'I've asked Hilary. She says we can use the chest freezer in their garage. As long as we place the boxes in black bags. She doesn't want her meat contaminated by the smell of fish.'

I nodded. We rented the surgery premises from Hilary and Andries who lived in a spacious apartment above the surgery. They had a chest freezer in the apartment and a second one in the garage, which was used only when they bought meat in bulk from a local farmer. Buying fish from the wholesaler would save us quite a bit. These days we were seldom without one or two penguins, usually more.

When Dr Long returned from leave, he decided that I should be assessed by a rheumatologist. There was a team of rheumatologists based at Tygerberg Hospital in Cape Town and he made an appointment for me.

'Your appointment is for Thursday at 7.30 in the morning.

It's a bit early but it's the only opening they had on that particular day.'

'It should be all right.'

Our friends Roger and Gail invited us to spend a few days with them. Since we had last seen them they had bought a smallholding on the mountainside near Scarborough.

We arrived in Cape Town on the Wednesday afternoon and that evening, after supper with Roger and Gail, I set the alarm for five o'clock the next morning.

Nic was less than thrilled at being woken when it was still dark and showed a distinct lack of cooperation when it came to eating his breakfast and allowing us to dress him. By the time we set off for the hospital, Dave and I were both feeling harassed.

We sped along the deserted road in the semi-darkness, but as the bakkie climbed the hill just beyond Silvermine, there was a muffled noise and it slewed to one side.

'Oh bugger!' Dave exclaimed.

'What?'

'We have a flat tyre. A blow-out I think.'

We arrived at Tygerberg Hospital at 8.30, one hour late. Directed to a room on the third floor, we flung ourselves into the lift and when the doors creaked open, we raced down a long corridor to the Rheumatology Department.

I lurched through the door and stumbled up to the counter.

'Good morning, I have an appointment to see Professor Bennett,' I gasped breathlessly.

The sister behind the counter stared at me.

'I'm sorry we're late, we had a blow-out.'

She looked confused. 'An appointment with Professor Bennett?'

'Yes.'

'What time is your appointment?'

'It was for 7.30.'

'There must be some misunderstanding. Professor Bennett will only be in at eleven today.'

My appointment was for 11.30. Dave and I decided to wait at the hospital, fearing that if we left the premises we might be late again.

Out of all the other days in the year, Nic had chosen that day to be impossible and we spent three hours trying to keep him away from lifts, stairwells and banisters.

Just after 11.30 I was shown into Professor Bennett's consulting room. I sat quietly while he read the referral letter and the lab reports. When he had finished, he looked up. 'So you have lupus.'

'Yes.'

'I see you have the Lupus Mask.'

'Pardon?'

'The mask. Over your cheekbones and nose.'

'I don't have a mask.' I stared at him.

'Yes, you do.'

'No, I don't.'

'Have a look,' he said, reaching into a drawer and handing me a small mirror.

I stared at my reflection. There were two spots of high colour on my cheekbones.

'That's not a mask,' I protested. 'I'm just flushed.'

'It's known as *the Lupus Mask*,' he smiled patiently.

'Well, it wasn't there this morning!'

If he had spent three hours trying to keep Nic occupied, he would also be flushed, I thought indignantly.

He examined me and drew blood for tests. While we waited for some of the results, he explained the many facets of the disease and the treatments available. I absorbed what he was telling me, gradually building up a picture of this disease I knew so little about. This wolf I was running with.

As I was leaving, he said I was welcome to telephone him at any time if I needed more information. More than ten years were to pass before I did.

Back at home, I decided it was time to stop the anti-inflammatory medication. To me, the tablets seemed to become less effective the longer I used them and they made me feel tired. I applied for the three weeks' leave due to me, stopped taking the tablets and started walking.

Once again the dogs and I were up and on the beach before dawn. On the first day they stood watching me curiously, puzzled by my slow pace as I limped across the sand.

'*Why doesn't she run?*' Mandy grunted at Whippy. '*At this rate it's going to take for ever.*'

'*I don't think she can.*'

At the end of the first week I started jogging. A very slow jog, but a jog nevertheless. Each day I tried to increase my pace and the distance covered.

Early one morning, halfway through the third week, as we moved along the waterline, sea mist swirling around us, I realised that my body was moving fluidly and swiftly.

And as my feet flew across the sand, suddenly Philby was in my head, eyes glinting green sparks as he smirked: '*You see, I told you. Don't worry about it. Just shut up and run.*'

I had been back at work for a few days, when Hilary popped in to see me. She said she'd had a rather unnerving experience at the weekend.

'What happened?' I asked.

She told me.

On Saturday evening, she had removed a plastic packet containing what she thought was a leg of lamb from the freezer in the garage. She placed the packet on a large tray and left it overnight on a shelf in her kitchen to defrost.

On Sunday morning, before she and Andries set off to play golf, she buttered the roasting pan and switched the oven on to preheat. When it was ready she lifted the plastic packet from the tray and upended it over the roasting pan. A large dead cat slid out into the pan.

'It was a ginger cat.'

'Oh God, Hilary! How did a dead cat end up in your freezer?'

'I'm not sure. But I think you should have a word with Dave.'

'I will. I'm so sorry!'

'Well, where was I supposed to put the cat?' Dave protested, when I confronted him that evening.

'Not in Hilary's freezer, for a start. Whose cat was it?'

'I don't know. It was found dead next to the main road. I thought the owners might come looking for it.'

'Hilary says Andries has gone right off roast lamb.'

'I was only going to leave it there for a few days.'

To the Heart of the Matter

The average lifespan of a greyhound is about thirteen years. Whippy was only eight when she died.

The first sign that there was something amiss came one evening when I returned from the library. It had been a glorious day, still and sunny, and on a sudden impulse, I decided to take the dogs to the beach.

'Come on,' I said to them. 'Let's go for a walk.'

Mandy, Arrow and Flenny jumped up, barking excitedly, and rushed outside. Whippy stood in the middle of the sitting room, looking at me with a strange expression on her face.

'Come, Whippy,' I said and walked out on to the veranda and across the lawn to the driveway. At the gate I paused and turned. She was standing on the veranda watching me.

'Whippy, what's the matter?' I asked. 'Don't you want to come for a walk?'

She shot me an apologetic look and turned and walked back inside the house. Puzzled, I stood for a moment gazing after her. It was unheard of for Whippy to miss a walk on the beach. The other three were already across the road and with a faint sense of unease, I strolled after them.

'Whippy wouldn't come to the beach this evening,' I told Dave when he arrived home.

'Whippy?' he looked surprised.

'Yes.'

Dave examined her, and as he ran his hand over her gammy leg, she yelped. The next day he took her into the surgery and X-rayed the leg. That evening, looking grim, he handed me the X-rays.

'It looks like bone cancer.'

'Oh no.'

'I'm sending the X-rays to a specialist radiologist in Pretoria for a second opinion.'

'Osteosarcoma,' the radiologist told Dave. 'The prognosis is poor. By the time one detects it, it has usually metastasised to the lungs.'

Dave sent the X-rays to a professor at Onderstepoort. Amputation was an option, he said. It would give Whippy an extra six months. If she was lucky. Left untreated, she would have one to three months.

Dave phoned a group of radiologists in Port Elizabeth to enquire about radiation therapy. There were no facilities for animals, they said, and chemotherapy was unlikely to help. It had never proved very effective for bone cancer.

'Dave, we can't put her through an amputation,' I said. 'Not with her sensitivity to pain. Not for just six months.'

'No,' he agreed. 'It would take her almost that long to recover fully from the operation. And we don't know to what extent the cancer has already spread.'

We agonised over what to do. The temptation was there to amputate. But we knew that to do so would be for us, and not for Whippy. We loved her so much, we couldn't bear the thought of losing her. But at the same time, we also knew that Whippy's pain threshold was extremely low. Over the years even a minor injury, like a gash on the leg from running into a branch or rock, had caused her severe distress. She feared pain, because she had experienced too much of it too early in life.

We decided to put her on strong painkillers and we made a soft bed for her in the corner of our bedroom, next to our bed. She seemed content to lie around for most of the day. When I came home from the library, I'd take her out into the garden to do her business and she'd amble around sniffing at the grass and flowers.

We gave her as much love as we could, secretly hoping that love could heal where medication couldn't. For several weeks she was fine.

Then one day we noticed her flinch when Nic bumped into our bed. He hadn't touched her, but she was obviously afraid that he might. At around the same time the expression in her eyes changed subtly. As if she was looking inwards, not outwards. Dave increased the dosage of painkillers and she responded immediately. But we knew that time was running out and we watched her closely for any signs of discomfort or distress.

After a few weeks on the higher dosage, she began passing blood in her stool and Dave said it was time to make a decision.

And choose a day.

It was so hard. Tomorrow was always better.

One morning we arranged for Nic to sleep over with Dodo and Bill. That evening Dave lifted Whippy gently on to our bed. We hugged and stroked her and gave her a bowl of warm milk, unable to believe that this was our last evening together. Finally, I lay down behind her, cuddling her to me and whispering into her ear, as Dave tried to find a vein through his tears.

When it was over, we lay holding her between us, sobbing brokenly.

Three months later, Dave discovered a suspicious mass in Mandy's abdomen. She had been slightly subdued since Whippy's death and we had assumed that she was grieving. But it was more than that.

Dave performed a laparotomy and found that the cancer had spread to the liver and kidneys. It was inoperable. He injected the euthanase while she was still under anaesthetic.

I had taken the afternoon off, and suspecting what he might find, Dave had placed a 'Closed' sign on the door of the rooms.

Afterwards, leaving Dave and Johannes to clear the theatre, I stumbled into the waiting room, blinded by tears.

An elderly gentleman and a dog were standing at reception. When I saw them, I mumbled hastily, 'I'm sorry we're closed.'

'The name is Beaumont,' he said. 'I read the notice and I hate to trouble.' He paused, taking in my tears. 'But I have a problem.'

I glanced down at the dog. Apart from being thin, it appeared healthy.

'I'm afraid we are closed,' I said firmly. 'Can you come back tomorrow?'

'You don't understand. This is not my dog. I found her on my veranda this morning and I don't know what to do with her.'

'Can't you try and find her owners?'

'I've walked the neighbourhood flat, from house to house. Nobody recalls having seen her in the vicinity before.'

I stared at the dog who looked back at me warily. She was obviously a German Shepherd cross, but instead of being black and tan, her coat was brown with flecks of black and gold. The eyes gazing at me were a yellowy topaz and there was a lean, mean look to her. She looked more like a wolf than a dog.

'We only have one large cage,' I explained. 'We can't really tie it up with a stray. Can't you keep her at home until her owners can be traced?'

'I have my doubts about her owners,' he said. 'I think she's been mishandled. She's very nervous, especially of children. She almost bit my grandson when he tried to pat her. He's staying with us for three weeks and I can't keep her while he's with us.'

I approached the dog slowly, holding out my hand. She stiffened and watched my approach with hackles raised. Murmuring soothing words, I reached out to stroke her but she flinched away.

'OK,' I sighed. 'We'll keep her here until you find her owners or another home for her.'

He assured me that he would do his utmost.

I held on to the dog as he left and called out to Johannes. As the theatre door opened and Johannes stepped out, the dog leapt forward with a venomous snarl. The door slammed shut and Johannes' face disappeared as quickly as it had appeared.

'That's very naughty of you,' I addressed the dog sternly, 'Johannes is a friend.'

Her lips lifted in an evil grin and I almost thought I detected gleam of laughter in those yellow eyes. Was it my imagination or did this dog have a sense of humour?

Losing both Whippy and Mandy within the short space of three months was absolutely devastating.

After Whippy's death, Dave and I carried our grief separately, deep inside, unable to talk about it. Pooling our grief would have made it unbearable. It was just too much. I'd return from work each day to be confronted afresh by the realisation that Whippy wasn't there to greet me.

And then Mandy. After her death I avoided going to the surgery for a while.

One evening, two weeks after she had died, Dave strode into the house in a very bad mood.

'That BLOODY dog!' he burst out.

'What dog?'

'That bloody miserable stray. The one you took in.' He gazed at me accusingly.

'Oh, is she still at the surgery?'

'Of course she's still there. Who would take her? Obviously her owners dumped her. They drove here from another town, opened their car door and shoved her out.'

'Don't exaggerate. What has she done?'

'Well,' he said sarcastically, 'she's merely attempted to bite every client who has the temerity to enter our door. Not the animals, you understand. Just the owners. The people who pay us.'

'But Dave, shouldn't she be in the big cage?'

'I need the big cage for sick animals.'

'I'm sorry. I suppose it's my fault for taking her in.'

'I've tried everything,' he continued. 'I've scolded her. I've hit her with a rolled-up newspaper. I tried closing her in the back of the bakkie during the day.'

'That was a good idea.'

'It didn't work. Each time somebody passed she'd launch into a mindless barking frenzy.'

'Oh dear.'

'I tried parking the bakkie across the road, hoping that

the noise of her hysterical barking wouldn't be audible in the consulting room.'

'And?'

'The couple who live across the road complained.'

'Oh.'

'It's not just the barking. She jumps up and down clicking her claws on the metal cab. The sound effects are quite frightening. By the time we home this dog, we'll be lucky if we have any clients left.'

'Maybe I should take her for a walk every day after work,' I suggested. 'If I can give her a bit of training, she might be easier to home.'

'Huh,' Dave snorted cynically.

The next afternoon when the library closed, I collected Nic from Dodo and Bill and on the way home I stopped in at the surgery.

'I'm going to take a dog for a walk,' I told Nic. 'You must wait here with Dad.'

'Why can't I come with you?'

'Because the dog doesn't like children.'

'Why?'

'I don't know. Perhaps a child hurt her.'

'Why?'

'Look Nic, I don't have all the answers.'

'Why not?'

'Never mind.'

The bakkie was parked outside the waiting room door and as we walked past it, ferocious barking and clicking broke out and the vehicle rocked violently. As we stepped into the waiting room, the consulting room door burst open and Dave rushed out, clutching a syringe filled with green fluid. Euthanase was green.

As he brushed past me I said, 'Dave, where are you going

with that?'

He ignored me and strode towards the bakkie. I ran after him.

'Dave, what are you doing?'

'I've had enough. It's no good, I'm going to have to euthanase her.'

'Why?'

'She's just bitten a man. He's threatening to sue.'

'Calm down, just calm down. Let's go inside and discuss it. You can't make a rational decision when you're in such a state.'

Eventually he calmed down sufficiently to tell me the story.

Earlier that afternoon, while he was busy preparing drapes and instruments for a bone op the next day, Dave had realised that he needed Pratleys putty for the external fixation of the pins. There was a gap between consultations and he decided to nip off to the hardware store. Because he was in a hurry, he didn't have time to transfer the stray dog from the back of the bakkie into the cage, so he took her with him.

'I was standing at the counter of the hardware store,' he said, 'when I happened to glance out at the bakkie.' As he watched, a well-dressed, middle-aged man stepped off the pavement and walked between the bakkie and the car parked next to it. As the man drew level with the back window of the bakkie, in a lightning flash of slavering canines, the stray's snout shot out and gripped the man behind the neck.

'She struck like a snake,' Dave said.

'OH NO!'

'I rushed out to help, but when the man screamed, she released him and whipped back into the bakkie.'

'What did he say?'

'Nothing at first. He was speechless, almost apoplectic. And then he went off about suing me. I apologised and told him that it wasn't my dog. But he said if it wasn't my dog what was it doing in the back of my vehicle?'

'He had a point.'

'Yes, well . . . anyway, she didn't actually pierce his skin. There was no blood, it was just a bit red. When I pointed this out to him, he was quite nasty. He said it was immaterial. He said it would be a cold day in hell before he accepted being bitten in the neck when he was innocently going about his business.'

'Dave, it must have been rather unnerving.'

'And embarrassing too. I didn't bother to go back for the Pratleys. I'll have to get it tomorrow.'

Leaving Nic with Dave, I took the stray down to the beach. She was obviously unused to a lead and she bucked and kicked all the way there. It was like walking a bronco. Fortunately the beach was deserted and I removed the lead and allowed her to walk free. Instead of bounding away as I half-expected, she remained at my side, glancing up at me every now and again as if seeking approval.

'You're such a good girl,' I cooed and she wagged her tail ecstatically, until her entire body was wagging along with it.

On the way back to the surgery she didn't buck at all. The following afternoon she walked sedately on the lead as if she'd been doing it all her life.

On the third day, I took her to the beach off-lead, telling her to 'heel'. She did. By the end of the week, all I needed to do was make a circle in the air with my forefinger and immediately she would fall in behind me. She was SO clever. And she LOVED Nic.

We decided to name her 'Beau'. It went very nicely with Arrow, we thought.

To the Heart of the Matter

On her way to the surgery early one morning, Jenny came across a kitten walking sedately down the middle of the road just opposite the cottage. The road was deserted. There was no sign of a mother cat or an owner and Jenny picked up the kitten and brought it to us.

She was pitch-black with sea-green eyes and very tiny.

'How old do you think she is?' I asked Dave.

'Five weeks, maybe six weeks at the most.'

'She's so small to be walking along the road on her own. Where do you think she came from?'

'I don't know. There's a colony of feral cats living in the dunes but if she came from there I'd expect her to be quite wild and she's not.'

I gazed at the kitten who lay curled up in Dave's arms, purring happily.

'Jenny says if we can keep her for a while, she'll find her a home,' he said.

When Pushcat had moved in with us Nic had experienced difficulty in pronouncing 'Push' and so he'd called her 'Cat'. When he saw the black kitten, he named her 'Othercat'.

Othercat settled in beautifully. Fluffy's maternal instincts emerged from their coma and from the first day she took Othercat under her wing. Overnight, Nuggie and Carrots were transformed into two kindly old uncles, who handed out advice at the drop of a hat. Carrots decided to teach her everything he knew about guns. It took two days. Nuggie exposed her to poetry.

'Sit still for a moment and listen to this,' he'd say with a diffident cough. *'Actually it's one of my own.'*

Shortly after Othercat's arrival, Hilary came to see me at the library.

'Andries and I are going to Cape Town for three weeks.'

'Oh, that's nice.'

'Yes. Chrystal, I wonder if you would store this leg of lamb in your freezer compartment at home?'

'Of course,' I said, taking the packet from her.

'The freezer in the apartment is empty and we've decided to leave it off while we're away.'

'But why don't you put it in the garage freezer?'

She told me.

Earlier that day she had popped in to the surgery, carrying the leg of lamb in the plastic packet. Dodo was behind reception, working on vaccination reminders. Hilary explained that she and Andries would be away for three weeks and that she wanted to leave the apartment freezer off.

'Dodo, I'm going to put this leg of lamb in the garage freezer,' she said. 'I want you to know so that it doesn't get mistaken for something else.'

'Fine, fine,' Dodo nodded. Then, as Hilary turned to leave, Dodo called out, 'Just don't put it on top of Mandy.'

Hilary froze. She swung round to face Dodo.

'Mandy? What's Mandy doing in the freezer?'

'Oh,' Dodo shrugged, 'Dave is still deciding where to bury her.'

Othercat had been with us for two and a half months when Jenny announced that she'd found a very good home for her.

'But we're all so fond of her now,' I protested, when Dave informed me.

'Yes I know, but Jenny says this young couple are very

keen. And as their only cat she'd get far more attention than she would here.'

In the end we let her go. Fluffy sank into a deep melancholia and took to wandering around aimlessly, muttering about being old and worthless.

'What's the matter with her?' Dave asked.

'She's missing Othercat.'

Carrots, on the other hand, was fairly philosophical.

'There wasn't much more I could teach her really,' he explained.

But poor old Nuggie was devastated.

'We'd just started on The Ancient Mariner,' he protested. *'I've prepared notes and everything.'*

'I'm sorry. We didn't think it fair to keep her when we have five cats and they don't have any.'

'I've spent SO much time and effort nurturing a love of poetry in her,' he moaned. *'And now it's all for NOTHING.'*

'It's not for nothing. You've given her a very good base to build upon.'

'But what about all my notes?' he whined. *'Now there's no one to teach.'*

'Teach one of the others. What about Pushcat?'

The next day Nuggie had a black eye and I realised that Pushcat had been an unfortunate choice.

'If she wants to live in a cultural desert she's welcome,' he remarked bitterly. He spent the week it took for the black eye to fade closeted in the bathroom, composing. An epic apparently. Something about an ancient harridan.

Subterranean Rumblings

The scream rose up from my toes, gathering momentum as it sped towards the frozen rictus of my mouth. I knew it was the last scream left in my body. After this there would be only dregs.

'BRUNNNNOOOOOoooooo . . .'

It sailed across the main road to the stop sign, where Bruno was busy savaging the tyres of a silver-grey Mercedes.

As the sound faded and died, the dark-tinted driver's window slid down silently and a clenched fist shook the air.

'He's not my dog,' I croaked as the vehicle accelerated, floating past me. They don't call them 'Silver Clouds' for nothing, I thought, watching a hysterical Knersers hurtle down the road after it. I made no attempt to call him. It wasn't even an option.

Beau stood at my side, glaring across the road at a jubilant Bruno, her lips curled in disapproval.

'Yes, he's bloody naughty,' I hissed. 'I've a good mind to give him a hiding. Him and bloody little Knersers.'

Knersers lived one block away from us up the hill. He was a cross schipperke/wire-haired terrier with a springy charcoal coat and an overshot jaw. Fish-jawed, Dave called it. 'He also has a leaking heart valve.'

'Well, I wish it would go and leak elsewhere,' I remarked bitterly.

Knersers and Bruno were making my life a misery. Neither of them were ever taken for walks on the beach by their respective owners and for some time I had noticed them watching us when we set off in the morning – watching with envious eyes.

Then one morning they were waiting at the gate.

'Ah, are you two joining us this morning?' I asked. They wagged their tails excitedly and gambolled on ahead.

We descended the steps on to the sand and Bruno paused on the bottom step to gaze into the distance. Following his gaze I spotted a woman further down the beach. At her feet a small fat dachshund was bouncing along happily. Before I realised what was happening, Bruno gave a deep 'WOOF' and took off. With Knersers after him.

'Stop, Bruno! STOP!' I shouted, racing across the sand in their wake.

With one horrified look, the woman scooped the dachshund up and held it at shoulder level. By the time I reached them, Bruno was jumping up at her, trying to get at the dachshund, while Knersers was yapping frenziedly at her ankles. I grabbed Bruno by the scruff of his neck and dragged him back and, with a few well-aimed kicks, I managed to dislodge Knersers from the woman's ankles.

'I'm sorry,' I panted breathlessly. 'I really didn't expect them to behave in this way.'

Still holding the dog aloft, the woman drew herself up to her full height.

'Vicious dogs should be walked on a lead,' she stated icily, glaring at me.

'They're not my dogs,' I explained. 'They followed me here.'

Without another word, she turned and stalked off down the beach, stumbling slightly under the weight of the dachshund. I opened my mouth to call after her and then shut it again. It was pointless. She obviously didn't believe me.

I decided to abandon my jog and turned back towards the steps with Beau, Arrow and Flenny trailing after me despondently. As we crossed the main road Bruno and Knersers veered off to chase a builder's truck, the back of which was filled with workmen. The catcalls and jeers of the workmen seemed to spur them on to greater efforts.

The next morning they were waiting at the gate again and sprang up enthusiastically at the sight of us.

'Come in, come in,' I said with a welcoming smile and as they rushed in, we nipped out and I slammed the gate shut. Ignoring their frustrated howls, we sprinted across the road and down the grass verge towards the beach.

For all their faults, Bruno and Knersers were fast learners. They never waited at the gate for us again. Not even once.

They skulked around corners and lurked behind bushes and when we were halfway to the beach, they would sweep past triumphantly, attacking everything in sight. The charge of the heavy brigade.

After several weeks of daily embarrassment, I approached Knersers' owners in desperation with a request that they try and keep him closed in until after six o'clock in the morning. Sometimes it worked and sometimes it didn't.

I bought a lead for Bruno and made it clear to him that he could only accompany us on lead. Every now and again his naughtiness would get the better of him and he would bound away before I could affix the lead to his collar. But it was only every now and again. And only after an inner battle. Walking with us on a lead made him feel as if he belonged. And he so badly wanted to belong.

We had been living at the cottage for two years when Dave and I began thinking of buying our own plot. Being so close to the surgery, the cottage was very convenient but it was also very small. Added to this was the fact that our relationship with Mrs Kowalski had deteriorated somewhat in recent months. There were two reasons for this – Nic's creativity and Dave's way with words.

Carmen had given Nic a large packet of plasticine for his birthday. I was less than enthusiastic when Nic removed the wrapping paper.

'I'm not sure this is a good idea,' I murmured.

'Chrystal, kids love plasticine. They need to express their creativity.'

Nic expressed his creativity on the external walls of the cottage. And Mrs Kowalski was not thrilled about this.

'You'll have to repaint the walls,' she said disapprovingly, on one of her regular inspections.

Shortly after this we sprang a leak. Over a period of two weeks we had become increasingly aware of the sound of running water in the bathroom without being able to establish the source. When we received the electricity and water account, both were extremely high.

'Look at this!' I wailed in dismay.

'It must be a hot water leak,' Dave said, studying the statement.

He approached Mrs Kowalski, who was responsible for organising repairs of this nature. She came over to inspect the bathroom.

'There is no leak,' she stated emphatically. 'There is no sign of running water.'

'If you listen carefully, you can hear water running all the time,' Dave pointed out.

'That's the toilet cistern.'

'No, it's not. It's a different sound entirely.'

She said she could not give permission for pipes to be dug up on such a flimsy suspicion.

'But what about our electricity and water consumption?' Dave asked, his voice rising in frustration.

She called in a friend of hers who was a handyman. After running a cursory eye over the bathroom and tapping the external pipes, he said there was no leak.

'What do we do now?'

'I don't know. If she won't give permission, our hands are tied.'

When the next electricity and water account arrived the amount owing was mind-boggling.

'This is ridiculous!' Dave exclaimed. The following morning he discovered that the ground against the external bathroom wall was hot beneath the grass.

'It's underground and definitely a hot water pipe.'

'Well, will you speak to Mrs Kowalski? I'm running a bit late.'

Thirty minutes later, the telephone rang in the Library. It was Mrs Kowalski. Without any preamble, she burst out angrily, 'I'm giving you people notice. I want you out of the cottage by the end of the month.'

'But why?' I asked helplessly.

'Your husband has just been extremely rude to me.'

'What did he say?'

'When I told him there was no leak, he said that one of us was a fool and it wasn't him.'

'I'm sorry. He's upset about the electricity and water account.'

'I've never been so insulted in all my life.'

'Mrs Kowalski, this morning there was steam rising from the grass growing against the bathroom wall.'

'Steam?'

'Yes.'

After a while she calmed down and agreed to withdraw the notice if Dave apologised. She said she would call in a plumber.

The plumber arrived on Saturday morning when Nic and I were home. He had only one leg.

'Where's his other leg?' Nic asked, as we stood in the bathroom watching him check the geyser.

I rolled my eyes at Nic.

'Why are you looking at me like that?'

'I'm not looking at you.'

'Yes, you are. Mom, where's his other leg?'

'Come, let's go and play in the garden.'

'Was it a shark?'

The leak was eventually traced to the hot-water piping laid under the bathroom floor.

In passing, Dave mentioned to one of his clients, a lawyer, that we were interested in buying a plot. During the next few weeks he took us to see several. The one we both liked bordered a gorge which formed part of a nature reserve. But it was too far from the centre of town for a veterinary practice.

If we built we would have to run the practice from the same premises. We couldn't afford to do otherwise. The lawyer suggested we view an old house near the centre of town. It might be cheaper than building ourselves, he said.

We arranged to meet him at his office after work one evening, but when we arrived he was out. His partner Alex apologised, saying that he'd been called away urgently.

'Which house was it that you wanted to see?'

We told him.

'I'll take you,' he offered. On the way to the house we chatted and he mentioned that there was a house for sale in our street.

'Which one?'

'They call it The Greenhouse.'

To this day, I cannot recall what the other house was like. We drifted through the rooms with only one thought in our minds – The Greenhouse.

The asking price was too high for us.

'Let's make him an offer,' Alex suggested. 'It's been on the market for some time now. Tony might be prepared to come down in price.'

To our delight, our offer was accepted. Tony planned to vacate The Greenhouse in three months' time, at the end of February. We would be able to move in on the first of March.

Just before Christmas, Dave broached the subject of acquiring another dog.

'Mrs Hilary's Dobermann had puppies a few weeks ago, they're really beautiful.'

'But Dave, we already have three dogs. And Bruno is desperate to come and live with us.'

'He belongs to Tony.'

'I think Tony would be quite happy for us to take him.'

'I'm sure. Look, Chrystal, you have to admit that Bruno is

a bit of a handful. He's never been trained. It would be far better to get a puppy and train it from the start.'

'I suppose so.'

I knew that Dave was still missing Mandy terribly, especially during the day. Beau was persona non grata at the surgery and neither Arrow nor Flenny were madly keen on spending their days there. They preferred to stay at home, lolling around on beds and couches. Dave needed a companion, a dog who would take on Mandy's role.

He brought Jade home on Christmas Eve. She was stunning, her coat a sleek jet-black and tan. Then I noticed her tail.

'What's happened to her tail?'

'What do you mean?'

'It's so short.'

'It's been docked. It's meant to be short.'

'Surely not that short.'

We looked down at the puppy, who promptly squatted and prepared to piddle on the sitting room carpet.

'There's nothing wrong with her tail,' Dave said, picking her up hastily. 'I docked it myself.'

'Dave have you seen Bruno lately?'

'No, I haven't. Not for the last week.'

'Nor have I. It's a bit strange, don't you think?'

'Maybe Tony's keeping him in.'

'Hmmm.'

That afternoon after work, I stopped in at The Greenhouse. Tony's domestic worker Agnes opened the door. She said he wasn't home.

'How is Bruno?' I asked. 'We haven't seen him for a while.'

'Bruno is chained up.'

'Oh. Why?'

'The lady who lives around the corner is complaining. She says he's digging up her garden.'

I nodded. 'Could I say hello to him?'

Agnes led me to the back garden where Bruno was lying forlornly in the middle of a patch of lawn, his collar attached to a chain anchored to a large wooden stake.

'Bruno, my BOY!' I called out and he jumped up, wagging his short tail. When I asked if I could take him for a short walk, Agnes appeared reluctant, so I left.

The next day was a Saturday. I went back to The Greenhouse and this time Tony answered the door himself.

'Hello Tony, I was wondering if I could take Bruno down to the beach?'

'Of course,' he said. 'Come in. Bruno needs the exercise.'

'You won't have to chain him up at your new house, will you?'

'I'm not taking him to the new house.'

'Oh, why not?'

'He's too destructive. I'm trying to find a home for him. A farmer who needs a guard dog is coming to look at him tomorrow.'

'A guard dog? Will he chain him up?'

'No, but he'll be kept in a run. Because of the sheep.'

On the beach I watched Bruno bound across the sand after Beau. He was such a powerhouse of energy and exuberance; the thought of him spending the rest of his life confined to a run was unbearable.

'You must speak to Tony,' I said to Dave that evening.

'Why?'

'He wants to give Bruno to a farmer. As a guard dog.'

'Maybe it's for the best. There'll be plenty of space on a

farm. Bruno will be in his element.'

'He'll be kept in a run.'

'Are you sure?'

'That's what Tony said. Dave, can't we take him?'

'If we take him we're going to run into trouble with Mrs Kowalski. You know how she feels about Bruno. The garden of The Greenhouse isn't fully enclosed and we can't afford to enclose it at this stage. Not with the expense of building alterations.'

Dave was right; we couldn't afford it. We had obtained quotes for converting the double garage into a surgery and had been horrified at the cost. Dave promised me he would speak to Tony the next day and try to convince him to take Bruno with him to his new house.

The next evening Dave arrived home just after I did.

'Tony is going to keep Bruno,' he announced proudly.

'Oh wonderful!' I sighed in relief. 'How did you manage that?'

'Until he moves.'

'Pardon?'

'He'll keep Bruno until he moves.'

'But what will happen then?'

'I said we'd take him.'

'What about Mrs Kowalski?'

'Bugger Mrs Kowalski.'

As I unlocked the library door, the telephone rang and dropping my handbag on to the counter, I rushed to answer it.

'Hello, Chrystal.' It was Hilary.

'Hello, Hilary.'

'Look, I thought I must tell you. I've just passed Dave driving through town with a cat on top of the bakkie.'

'WHAT!'

'It was spreadeagled on the roof of the canopy.'

'OH NO!'

'I waved to him and pointed, but he waved back and just kept going.'

It was Pushcat. She had taken to falling asleep on top of the bakkie.

We searched the route that Dave had travelled but there was no trace of her.

Three days later, on a Saturday morning, she limped into the house. She had a swollen hindleg but she was otherwise unhurt. Despite this, she was very bitter about the experience.

'All I did was lie down for a five-minute nap,' I overheard her telling the others, *'when suddenly I find myself hurtling along the main road. And of course he took that corner much too fast. It was by the grace of God that I missed the lamp post.'*

As I walked away, she was muttering something about 'Sleeping with one eye open in future . . .'

That evening I was sitting on the couch watching TV when I heard a vehicle stop outside. The dogs jumped up and rushed out, barking furiously. When I walked out on to the veranda, I saw two heads peering over the front wall. I strolled over to them and recognised them as the young couple who had adopted Othercat.

'Hello,' I said. 'How's Othercat? She must be quite big by now.'

'We've brought her back,' the young woman announced, flicking her long dark hair over her shoulders.

'Oh, why?'

'She doesn't fit in.'

'In what way?'

'We think she's evil.'

I gazed at them in astonishment.

Just then Dave walked up the drive.

'Hello,' he said, walking over to us. 'How's Othercat doing?'

'They've brought her back,' I muttered.

'Oh?' He looked surprised. 'Why, is there something wrong with her?'

'They think she's evil.'

Dave stared at them.

'She keeps peeing on our Persian carpet,' the young woman explained.

'Oh,' Dave nodded. 'Perhaps she has a urinary infection. But what makes you think she's evil?'

'We can't explain it, we just know. We're reborn, you know.'

They had brought her back in a small closed cardboard box. As Dave took it from them they mentioned that they had changed her name to Pookie.

We opened the box in our bedroom and as Dave reached in to lift her out, she cringed and hissed at him.

'I think we should just leave her alone for a while,' he said. 'Let her calm down.'

We closed the bedroom door and a while later when we went back to check, we found her huddled under our bed.

'What on earth has happened to her? She's terrified.'

'I don't know, but she's definitely been traumatised.

Othercat stayed under our bed for almost a week. She was so wild we couldn't touch her. We provided a litter tray and a bowl of water and pushed her meals in when it was time to eat. We decided to call her Pookie, hoping it would help. It didn't. She was a nervous wreck.

In the end it was Nuggie who succeeded in getting her out. He spent hours lying on the floor with his head stuck in under the bed, reciting poetry. By the end of the week I think she'd had enough.

'That sonnet sucks,' I overheard her say crossly one afternoon.

Gradually she overcame her fear and allowed us to stroke her again and, two weeks later, Dave managed to get a urine sample. She had a roaring infection and he put her on a course of antibiotics.

Dyed in the Wool

The Greenhouse had a sitting tenant. We only discovered this on the evening of the day we moved in.

He was big and black and his body was covered in scabs. Two tattered ears were arranged randomly on either side of his large scarred head and, in repose, his face sported two long, yellowed canines which protruded over his bottom lip. A thread of saliva dangled from each canine.

Exhausted after the move, Dave and I were sitting at the table which divided the kitchen from the sitting room area when he strolled in through the sliding doors, as if he owned the place. At a glance we could see that this was a cat who had been around the block a few times. And now the block was his.

Slightly taken aback, we watched him cruise past Nuggie and Carrots who were stretched out on the couch, discussing sleeping arrangements. Their conversation froze in mid-air when they saw him, their mouths dropping open in naked disbelief. As one they leapt down on to the floor.

'*Excuse me,*' said Nuggie pleasantly, tapping the black cat on the shoulder.

The cat's head whipped round. He never even gave them a chance to introduce themselves. He just laid into them.

Within seconds the air was thick with ginger fur and shrieks of pain.

In the seconds it took for us to react, Carrots lost a wedge of flesh from his left ear and Nuggie lay crumpled on the floor, his right eye swollen shut. Blood welled from four claw tracks across his nose. Scooping them up we rushed them into the bathroom.

'Where am I?' moaned Nuggie in a faint voice. *'What happened?'* he shook his head weakly, trying to focus with one eye.

'I think it was a Rottviolet,' sniffed Carrots, blood streaming down his face and dripping on to the tiles.

After cleaning and disinfecting their wounds, we decided to leave them in the bathroom on hot water bottles for a while, until they were out of shock.

When we returned to the sitting room, the black cat was sprawled on the rug before the TV cleaning his private parts.

'He's behaving as if he belongs here,' I mused. ' I wonder whose cat he is?'

'I don't know. Tony never mentioned a cat.'

Just then, Pushcat jumped in through the kitchen window and wandered over to us. The black cat paused in his ablutions to leer at her lasciviously.

'HellOOO Doll,' he smarmed.

The last 'l' of doll was still on his lips when she hit him. Her first blow took him on the side of the head and knocked the spit right off his canines. She followed through with a straight right that slammed him up against the sitting room wall. He slid down the wall in slow motion and as his paws touched solid ground his body exploded into action and he hurtled out into the night. Straight into the swimming pool.

He must have had swimming lessons because by the time we reached the sliding doors, he was heaving himself up on to the pool steps.

'Oh shame,' I said. 'Come, let me dry you off.'

With one sodden disillusioned look at us he slunk off into the garden, trailing his long sopping tail behind him.

He had won the cat fight. But lost the war.

When Dave spoke to Tony the next day we found out that his name was Gobbelino and that he came with the house. He was a stray that Jenny had adopted shortly before she sold the house. When he refused to settle at the cottage, Tony had agreed to take him in.

We shortened his name to Gobby. The fact that he was always dribbling had absolutely nothing to do with it, I told the other cats. When Dave examined him he discovered that apart from the sores on his body, he also had sores on his tongue and he put him on to treatment.

After the initial incident the atmosphere in the house remained distinctly tense for a few days.

'We have taken transfer, I presume?' Pushcat asked pointedly, within Gobby's hearing.

'Yes, of course.'

'Well, then, why is he still . . .?'

'Pushcat!'

'But . . .'

'THE SUBJECT IS CLOSED!'

Oddly enough, within a few days Nuggie and Carrots befriended him. I wasn't sure whether it was a case of forgive and forget, or whether they were still looking for the Rottviolet. I didn't ask. Some things are better left alone.

I felt very sorry for Gobby. Despite his aggressive macho image, physically he was very neglected and somehow I got the impression that he had had a rather rough and ready upbringing.

'Why does he slurp his food?' asked Seafood, one evening at

supper time.

'Never mind what he's doing. You concentrate on your own supper.'

'But why is HE allowed to chew with his mouth open?'

'Because he has a sore tongue, OK?'

'But . . .'

'SHUT UP AND EAT YOUR SUPPER!'

After the cramped conditions of the cottage, the new house was like a castle. There was so much space we didn't quite know what to do with it.

The original house was a square structure with a passage running down the middle. On one side of the passage lay the open-plan sitting room cum kitchen area, and on the other were two bedrooms and a bathroom.

The glass sliding doors at the end of the sitting room opened out on to the brick-paved pool area. Next door to the sitting room, Nic's bedroom had double glass doors which also opened out on to the pool area. Our bedroom was not part of the original building and had been added on only a few years before Jenny sold the house. Unlike the house which had plastered walls, the extension was built of dark wine-red facebrick.

Our bedroom was beautiful. It had a red facebrick floor and a pine log ceiling. The room was huge and had three French windows, one opening out on to the pool and the other two on to the garden.

The en suite bathroom was big enough to serve as a bedroom itself. It housed a light-green round sunken bath, a toilet, a bidet and a shower. The floor was its most unusual feature. One half was tiled in dark-green Italian tiles while the other half consisted of earth, covered by a layer of round white river stones. Two skylights were set in the log ceiling and a French window opened out on to a small walled garden, in the middle of which stood a three-tiered fountain.

Nic was thrilled when he discovered the bidet.

'Mom, LOOK,' he called. 'It's a basin specially for children.' Before I could stop him, he turned the tap on full blast and a jet of water shot into his face.

'It's meant for your other end,' I told him.

He was fascinated by the bidet and before long the bathroom was being frequented by a furtive trail of children. By the time their parents collected them, they all had one thing in common. They had the cleanest faces in town.

Prior to moving in we had measured the swimming pool and ordered a safety net from a supplier in Johannesburg. Dave and I had decided that it would be impractical to fence the pool, as the pool edge was a mere metre and a half away from the sliding doors of the sitting room.

Apart from this problem, we felt that a net would be safer and eliminate the risk of a gate being left open accidentally.

To our dismay, when we attempted to fit the net on the day we moved in, it was too small. The supplier had sent the wrong size. When we phoned them they said they were temporarily out of stock and estimated that it would take two weeks to get the right net to us.

Nic was five years old when we moved into The Greenhouse and he couldn't swim. Two very nerve-racking weeks followed, in which I dogged his every footstep.

'Mom, please stop following me.'

'Come with me, Nic, we're going to hang curtains.'

'I don't want to hang curtains. I'm playing with my cars.'

'Come anyway.'

'MO..OM.'

Late one afternoon, I was on my hands and knees packing a cupboard in the kitchen when I heard Dave call out that he was nipping up to his mom and dad to borrow a shifting spanner.

'Are you taking Nic with you?' I called back. The front door slammed shut and the next minute I heard the bakkie zoom off. Obviously he hadn't heard me. I paused for a moment and listened. The house was absolutely still. Nic must have gone with him. I went on packing.

Five minutes later there was a muffled *splash* from the direction of the pool. I jumped to my feet and stared out through the open door. Widening circles of ripples were moving from a point in the centre of the pool towards its edge. The dish in my hand crashed to the floor and shattered as I leapt forward.

Beau was there before me, barking hysterically as she peered into the deep end. A few centimetres below the surface, Nic was hanging suspended in the water, not moving. I dived in, spectacles and all, and as I grabbed him and heaved his head above the water he burst into shocked sobs. I swam to the side and as I staggered up the steps with him clutched in my arms, Beau squeaked with relief.

'It's all right, it's all right, you're safe now,' I reassured Nic above his wails. He howled even louder and pointed to the pool.

'What's the matter?' I asked.

'My BLANKEEEeee,' he wailed.

I turned to look at the pool. Nic's white satin-trimmed security blanket was descending gently into the depths of the deep end.

'Don't worry, I'll get it later. Let me dry you off first.' His mouth opened wide and before the sound could hit the airwaves, I said hastily, 'OK, OK, wait here, I'll get it for you,' and dived back into the water, still wearing my spectacles.

The safety net arrived two days later. Despite this, we knew we wouldn't rest easy until Nic had learned how to swim. We hit a brick wall when we tried to get him to put his head under the water. He said he'd done it once and it wasn't a fun experience.

One morning when two of his friends were visiting, I tossed a handful of silver coins into the shallow end.

'Whoever dives those out can keep them,' I said cunningly.

Within a week Nic was swimming like a fish.

Early one Sunday morning, three weeks after we moved in, there was a loud knock on the front door. Dave and I were sitting at the kitchen table drinking coffee. He was waiting for an emergency case to arrive.

'That must be them now,' I said. 'Finish your coffee quickly, I'll answer.'

I opened the door to find Mrs Kowalski standing on the steps. She was wearing a white suit and a round pink hat and she looked very smart.

'Morning,' I said. 'Gosh, you're looking very elegant.'

Without acknowledging my comment she hissed, 'That DOG has dug up my garden.'

'Which dog?'

'BRUNO,' she spat the words out, her face contorting on the consonants.

'Oh.'

'FOUR BEDS OF NEWLY PLANTED SEEDLINGS!'

'I'm terribly sorry.'

'I'm leaving for church now,' she said in a frigid voice.

'When I return I expect to find the seedlings replanted.'

'Of course, don't worry, I'll start immediately.'

Without another word she swung round and stalked off. From the back, even her hat looked angry.

The seedbeds resembled a building site. Deep pits and mounds of soil bore witness to the enthusiasm of Bruno's excavations. He had a tendency to throw his heart and soul into a project. The seedlings that were still visible above ground looked a tad battered and as I stared at them thoughtfully, I wasn't sure that replanting was the answer.

Before long, the heat of the sun was beating down and sweat streamed off me as I scraped and dug and patted soil around little plants that refused point-blank to stand upright. I bent over to shovel soil into a deep pit and when I straightened up Bruno was there. He had obviously tracked me down the road. He lifted a paw to help me dig and I yelled, 'GET OUT OF HERE, YOU SWINE!' He gambolled off playfully across the bed I had just finished and I was forced to go over it again with the rake.

When all four beds were finished, I grabbed Mrs Kowalski's hosepipe and gave them a good sprinkle. Then I left hurriedly.

Over the next few weeks Mrs Kowalski proceeded to make my life a misery. I'd arrive home from work and before I could even sit down and have a cup of tea, there would be a peremptory knock on the front door.

'Your dogs have messed on my lawn again. Kindly come and see to it immediately.' *Immediately* was enunciated in such a way that I knew there was no hint of an option here. No nice hot cup of tea lurking between the lines.

On a couple of occasions when I was late getting home, she'd walk down the road and deposit the faeces in our driveway.

Dyed in the Wool

'Can't we feed the dogs some kind of vegetable dye?' I asked Dave one evening.

'Dye! What on earth for?'

'Something that will dye their faeces bright blue or red.'

'Why would we want to do that?'

'Because I don't think it's our dogs messing on Mrs Kowalski's lawn. We have four large dogs and one small one and the faeces she's asking me to pick up are from a medium-sized dog.'

'Well then, refuse to do it.'

'Yes, but I need proof.'

We had a long discussion on the merits of cochineal as opposed to blue cake colouring but before we could implement the plan, matters came to a head.

The following afternoon when I went to collect Nic from Dodo and Bill, he was hot and feverish. They said he'd refused lunch and had spent the afternoon sleeping. It was pouring with rain and Bill held an umbrella over us as I carried Nic to the Beetle. On the way home he huddled miserably on the back seat crying and groaning that his head hurt.

The rain was still sheeting down when I parked in the road opposite our front door and as I lifted Nic from the vehicle, I saw Mrs Kowalski storming down the road towards us, obviously in a temper. Her face was red and blotchy and in a momentary loss of control, she snapped, 'Come and remove your dogs' SHIT from my lawn. NOW!'

'Mrs Kowalski, just give me a few minutes. Nic's quite ill and I need to get him in out of this rain.'

She launched into a tirade about people who allow their dogs to defile other people's lawns. Desperate to get Nic inside, I brushed past her.

'I'll be with you in a minute,' I said.

I popped Nic into his bed and gave him a dose of analgesic syrup.

'Just lie here quietly, I'll be back in a minute.'

'Mom, can't you stay with me for a while? My head really hurts,' he wept.

'I have to go and see Mrs Kowalski. I won't be long, I promise.'

Worried about leaving Nic alone, I went down the road and around the corner. Mrs Kowalski was standing in the doorway of her veranda, her arms folded across her chest. I glanced around the lawn, my vision hampered by the raindrops on my spectacles.

'Where is it?' I called out. She pointed towards the base of the front hedge where a single medium-sized stool was trying to conceal itself amongst a pile of dead leaves.

'Where's the spade?' I asked.

She bridled angrily. 'I am no longer prepared to allow my spade to be used for dog mess,' she said. 'You'll have to bring your own.' I stared at her for a long moment and then turned away and walked back to our house.

By the time I returned with the spade, I was sopping wet. As I stooped to scoop, she shouted, 'MAKE SURE YOU GET IT ALL.'

It was as if something in my head snapped. It went 'PINGGG . . .'

I straightened and turned to look at her.

'You know, you're right,' I nodded slowly. 'This IS shit. This is ABSOLUTE shit!' I walked over to her with the spade held out before me. 'Look at this,' I said coldly. 'We do not have a dog that will produce a stool of this size. THIS . . . IS . . . NOT . . . OUR . . . STOOL!'

'Well . . . ummm,' she stammered, looking taken aback. 'If your dogs aren't doing it, then who is?'

'There are several other dogs living in the vicinity. And what about your gentleman friend's cocker spaniel?'

'He doesn't live here.'

'Maybe not, but he visits every day. Look, Mrs K,' I said more calmly, 'if you have a genuine complaint, then we'll always be prepared to listen. But you know as well as I that, apart from Bruno, our dogs never venture on to your property.'

She stared at me silently.

'Anyway, please excuse me, I have a sick child to attend to,' I said and walked away, carrying the spade and its controversial contents.

I suspected that the whole exercise had very little to do with dog faeces. To my mind, it had everything to do with a leaking bathroom pipe.

A Whiff of Revolt

The thing we loved most about The Greenhouse was its garden. Tony had cut down several trees during his occupation, but despite this the garden was still wild and overgrown.

Steps led down from the brick-paved patio surrounding the pool to an area of mossy lawn. The lawn encircled a thicket of trees, the biggest of which was a gnarled, twisted milkwood. Below its spreading branches, shiny clusters of black berries lay scattered on the ground, forming a mushy layer underfoot. The milkwood was at least eighty years old, Jenny told us.

Indigenous creepers hung from the trees, snaking around trunks and branches and twisting to form thick brown monkey-ropes. On the ground between the trunks tumbles of moss-covered calcified rocks, embedded with seashells, lay piled upon each other. Years of dripping rain and dew had worn hollows in the rocks and in these hollows, tiny maidenhair ferns and glossy succulents had taken root.

A low tunnel through the thick undergrowth led to a small raised clearing in the centre of the thicket. Sitting in the clearing, one could hear the whiplash crack of waves breaking on to the shore and smell the sea-air mingled with the rich smell of rotting leaves.

Between our property and the one at the back, a flimsy wire fence was strung beneath a line of tall windblown pine trees. They slanted over the garden like protective giants.

A raised rockery dotted with bromeliads, bracken ferns, clivia and the odd bougainvillaea, lay against the overgrown hedge which separated our garden from our neighbour on one side.

On the opposite side we had two neighbours, as the double plot had been subdivided and a vibracrete wall erected along the boundary. Just inside the wall the fallen trunk of a large yellowwood lay draped under a curtain of black-eyed susan and morning glory. The brilliant orange and mauve flowers glowed like stars amidst the greenery. Against the corner of our bedroom wall, a flourishing ginger tree shed crisp fragrant blossoms on to the ground and the thick trunk of a willow curved up towards the roof.

The garden was a magical mystical place for children. There were so many nooks and crannies that when it came to Hide and Seek, the seeker would often become quite disheartened.

As the fumes engulfed me I gasped, swallowed convulsively and a piece of steak and a chip sailed down my throat, unchewed. Sitting alongside me, his fork poised in mid-air, Dave glanced at me curiously. As he opened his mouth to speak, the smell hit him and, flinging his fork down, he leapt to his feet and lurched towards the bathroom.

'Oh NO!' gagged Nic, tumbling from his chair with one hand clamped over his mouth as he stumbled after Dave.

'JADE, get out from under the table!' I exclaimed crossly,

nudging her body with my foot. 'Go outside.'

With a reproachful look, she heaved herself up and stalked out stiff-legged through the sliding doors. I grabbed a newspaper and fanned the air vigorously and reaching for the can of air freshener, I sprayed lavishly under the table.

'It's all right, you can come back now,' I called out to Dave and Nic.

They approached warily, peering under the table.

'It's OK, I've chased her outside.'

'Why does Jade let off such big farts?' asked Nic.

'Gaseous emissions,' I corrected hastily.

'Well, why does she let off such big gaseous emissions?'

'It's because her tail is too short.'

'Don't be ridiculous,' Dave snorted. 'Her tail has absolutely nothing to do with it.'

'Dave, if she had a longer tail it would act as a barrier. It would cushion the flow.'

'That's nonsense. It has nothing to do with the length of her tail. It has to do with her digestion,' Dave said firmly.

'If she carries on like this, we're going to have to go out and buy gas masks.'

'Mom, what are gas masks?'

'I'll give her some activated charcoal again,' Dave sighed.

We loved Jade dearly, but if there was one word in the English language to describe her, it was 'inconvenient'. Jade was an inconvenient dog.

At five months she was still not fully house-trained. In addition to this problem, she was highly strung and extremely difficult to discipline. Her mind seemed to shut down when it received a command. If we allowed her off-lead on the beach, she'd immediately race off wildly after the seagulls, ignoring our calls. Dave would hurtle after her screaming, 'JADE . . . JADE . . . JADE . . . COME BACK!' as he pursued her over rocks and into pools and through the municipal caravan park, watched by groups of curious campers. Nic and I and the other dogs would wait patiently on the sand. Eventually he'd reappear from amongst the tents and caravans, puffing and panting, sweat pouring off him as he dragged an unrepentant Jade by her collar.

'The dog has a single brain cell,' I observed. 'And squatting in the middle of it is a smirking seagull.'

'There's nothing wrong with her brain,' Dave said testily. 'She's just vying for dominance.'

Once we'd moved into The Greenhouse, we hired a builder to undertake the alterations to convert the double garage and storeroom into a surgery. It took him and his team just over a month and once the alterations were complete, we moved the surgery furniture and equipment to the new rooms.

Everything proceeded smoothly, until it came to moving the surgery cat. Be-Barp didn't want to be moved.

'I like it here where I am,' he said stubbornly.

The new tenants didn't really want a cat and we had to go over and fetch him three or four times a day, only to have him drift back again as soon as he thought we weren't looking. At suppertime I'd stand out on the pavement and call loudly, 'BE-BARP . . . BE-BARP . . . BE-BARP!'

'God, I feel like a fire engine,' I told Dave one evening.

'What do you mean?'

'Standing out on the pavement shouting, Be-Barp . . . Be-Barp. People are giving me some really funny looks. We should never have named the cat Be-Barp.'

'Nic named the cat.'

'Well, that's all very well, but he's not the one who has to stand out there calling.'

Shortly after this we acquired a parrot. An elderly couple

brought it in to Dave. They said it was plucking out all its feathers and biting at its leg until the blood flowed.

'Sometimes in the morning its cage is covered in blood,' the gentleman told Dave. 'We cannot cope, my wife is a nervous wreck.'

When Dave carried the cage into the house, I stared at the shivering featherless bird.

'What kind of bird is it?' I asked curiously.

'It's an African Grey.'

'It looks more like a Norwegian Blue to me.'

'It'll be fine once its feathers have grown back.'

'Why is it plucking them?'

'I'm not sure. It could be one of several reasons.'

'Maybe it's pining for the fjords,' I suggested. 'Does it have a name?'

'Yes. Stupid.'

'You don't have to call me that. I'm merely asking if the bird has a name.'

'Stupid is its name.'

'Oh.'

We decided to change his name to 'Stewey'. Stewey settled in very well and once we'd convinced the cats that he wasn't on the menu, we allowed him the freedom of the house and garden. We both disliked the idea of keeping a bird confined to a cage.

He'd spend his nights in the cage on our bedroom floor. In the morning we'd open the cage door and he'd clamber out and make his way across the room to the bed with his odd rolling gait, like a sailor who has been at sea for too long. He'd climb up on to the bed and settle comfortably on Dave's chest, where he'd sit plucking gently at Dave's beard. When we rose, he'd amble out through the French window and climb up into the potted hibiscus, where he spent most of his days.

Before very long, his feathers grew back and he became a very handsome parrot. At night when we placed the cover over his cage, he'd mumble sleepily, '*Night . . . night.*'

'Night . . . night, Stewey,' we'd say. 'Sleep tight.'

Frustrated by his lack of progress in training Jade, Dave decided that training would be better undertaken where there weren't any people around. Especially people in caravans and tents.

So very early one Sunday morning, we decided to take the dogs to the isolated beach across the Hippo River, where we'd often camped overnight.

The dogs were thrilled when they realised an outing was in the offing. They bounced and cavorted around the bakkie and when Dave opened the canopy door they leapt in, whining and squeaking excitedly.

They whined and squeaked all the way through the sleeping town, but just as we reached the outskirts the noise ceased abruptly. A short silence was followed by frenzied high-pitched barking. I peered through the glass between the cab and the back. I could see Beau and Arrow on one side, their heads wedged through the open sliding window. Opposite them, Bruno had forced the other window open and was hanging halfway out of the bakkie. From where I was sitting I couldn't see Jade and Flenny at all.

'There's something happening in the back,' I said. 'I think we should stop and check.'

Dave pulled over to the side of the road and climbed out. As he opened the door of the canopy, Beau, Arrow, Flenny and Bruno burst out and landed in a confused heap on the tar, expressions of pure desperation on their faces. Jade remained standing inside, looking slightly sheepish. As the stench of dog pooh billowed out into Dave's face, he reeled back clutching his nostrils. Jade's sphincter had done it again.

Using crumpled newspaper, we cleaned up as best we could and Dave scooped up sand from the side of the road and sprinkled it over the affected area. When it came to getting the dogs back into the bakkie, there was an atmosphere of general rebellion and Dave had to issue several loud commands.

Beau refused point-blank.

'I'm revolting,' she said. *'This far and no further.'*

'You're not revolting,' I corrected. 'It's revolting. The smell is revolting.'

'No,' she stated flatly, her mean yellow eyes flashing contemptuously. *'I'm revolting. Under no circumstances will I ever enter the back of a vehicle with that animal again.'*

We allowed her to squash into the front with us.

This was the first incident in a pattern that was to repeat itself time and time again. Dave tried trotting Jade up and down the road before setting off, hoping to get things moving before the trip. Sometimes it worked, sometimes it didn't.

Eventually the situation deteriorated to such an extent that if Jade leapt up into the bakkie first, the other dogs would mill around on the ground, staring up at her resentfully.

As I walked into the sitting room Pushcat ran past me, going in the opposite direction.

'Just wait till I lay my hands on him,' she seethed. *'Where's*

my hockey stick? This time I'm going to finish him off.'

'Lay your hands on who?' I called after her. 'Finish who off?'

Ignoring me, she disappeared into our bedroom.

'What's going on?' I asked Nuggie and Carrots who were sitting on the couch. Carrots glanced up from the gun catalogue he was paging through.

'It's Gobby.'

'He's begging again.' Nuggie shook his head sadly.

I opened the front door and strode outside and there he was. A pathetic sight, his fur clotted with bits of dried mud as he sat mournfully on the pavement, his empty food bowl at his side.

I stood for a moment watching him. There was only one ingredient missing from the scene. And that was a sign, a rough cardboard one containing the words:

Abandinned at berth

Plees hulp

I crept up behind him.

'Gobby, what on earth are you doing?'

He started guiltily and swung round to face me.

'Oh, it's you.'

'Yes.'

'Well, er, I thought . . . um . . . it would be nice to have a little bit extra . . . you know.'

'A bit extra what? Are you not getting enough to eat?' I asked, a veiled reference to the mummified mouse corpse I'd found him huddled over earlier that morning.

'I am, I am . . . it's not that . . . it's just, well . . . force of habit really,' he explained sheepishly.

'Gobby you don't need to beg any longer,' I said, sitting down next to him. 'You have a home and a family now and three meals a day. If you find you have too much time on your hands and have to resort to begging, then we'll organise some activities for you. What about a bit of reading?'

'*No, no,*' he said hastily. '*I wouldn't want you to go to any trouble on my behalf.*'

'No trouble,' I said. 'I have a lovely book entitled *We Are What We Eat*. You could start with that.'

'*No, it's all right. Really. I think I'm ready to give up begging now.*'

'Good. Now let's go inside and clean that mud off you.'

We went back inside to find Pushcat berating Seafood.

'*If you borrow something you must return it,*' she was saying loudly. '*Can you not remember where you left it?*'

Apparently Pushcat had been strolling down the road towards the house, with an ardent admirer in tow, when she spotted '*the cretin*' sitting on the pavement. '*I've never been so embarrassed in all my life.*'

'What did you do?'

'*I said we'd moved house again and just kept on walking.*'

Parrot Fashion

The cats settled into The Greenhouse without any fuss. They each developed their own routine. Gobby already had an established routine and frequented the alleyway just outside the kitchen door, where he'd curl up on the lid of the large rubber refuse bin. When the municipal refuse collectors came around twice a week, they were forced to lift him off in order to remove the black bag from inside the bin. I worried that he might be mistaken for rubbish and end up in a waste disposal unit somewhere.

'But why would they mistake him for rubbish?' Carrots asked naively. *'Anyone can see he's a cat.'*

'You know he's a cat, and I know he's a cat, but it may not be immediately obvious to an outsider.'

'But I still don't . . .'

'I'll explain some other time,' I said hastily. 'I think Nuggie's calling you.'

As Carrots wandered off, my eyes strayed through the kitchen window to Gobby who was lying on top of the bin as usual. I couldn't help thinking that he bore a strong resemblance to a fur wrap. An old black acrylic one, that someone had discarded.

Nuggie and Carrots alternated between watching TV and

lolling around the pool in deckchairs, debating the merits of guns as opposed to poetry. Carrots maintained that guns and poets had much in common. He said they both went off a lot.

Sometimes they'd abandon these pursuits to proffer advice on the hanging of curtains.

'A little bit to the right, I think,' murmured Nuggie, *'and a few more rings on that one.'*

'There, what do you think?'

'That's perfect.'

'Can we hang on them now?' Carrots chipped in eagerly.

'ABSOLUTELY NOT!'

'But . . . you said we could help with hanging on curtains.'

'Hanging OF curtains . . . OF!'

Seafood would disappear into the garden after breakfast and only reappear at suppertime, while Pushcat spent her days ratting (and chairing Hockey Club meetings in an empty plot just down the road). Pookie and Fluffy staked their claim to our bedroom, only venturing out to perform their ablutions.

As it happened, they didn't venture out as often as we would've liked. Before long we detected a smell of cat urine in our bathroom. Purely by chance I came upon them one day as Fluffy was demonstrating.

'You see, you just push one of these little stones aside and then when you're finished, you just push it back again.'

Soon we were having to lift river stones in order to replace the soil underneath and the term 'en suite' took on a deeper meaning. We couldn't scold them as Pookie was still extremely nervous and Fluffy had become very frail. After she was blown into the pool by a sudden gust of wind one Sunday afternoon, we kept a watchful eye on her. Her kidneys were failing and we knew her time was near.

But when the loss came, it wasn't Fluffy.

As I walked through the sitting room on my way to make tea early one morning, I glanced over at the couch. Carrots and Nuggie were still fast asleep. Or so I thought. Then I stopped. There was something strange about the way Nuggie was lying. He was stretched out awkwardly and as I reached out and laid my hand on his body, I knew. I picked him up and saw that his tongue was protruding from the other side of his mouth. It was blue.

'DAVE!' I shouted, running into the bedroom with Nuggie in my arms. 'WAKE UP . . . I don't think Nuggie's breathing!'

We rushed him into the theatre and while Dave inserted an endotracheal tube, I switched the oxygen on. Our efforts were in vain, we were unable to revive him.

Later that morning Dave performed a post-mortem. He discovered that Nuggie's heart was the size of a kitten's. It had been compressed by a lobe of his liver which had pushed through a herniated diaphragm into his chest cavity. This must have occurred when he was still very young.

'The fact that he survived this long with a heart that size, is a miracle,' Dave told me.

When he said this, I suddenly remembered our walks in the veld in Swaziland. Often, halfway through a walk, Nuggie would stand up on his hindlegs, asking to be carried and I'd sling him over my shoulder and carry him home. The writing had been on the wall. I simply hadn't read it.

We buried him under the milkwood, a fitting place for a poet, we thought. With Carrots at my side, I watched Dave shovel soil into the hole and it occurred to me that Nuggie's heart may have been physically small, but in spirit it was huge. He had been a gentle giant of a cat and the grief I felt at his passing was in many ways a gentle grief. This time around I didn't howl or sob, I simply ached with sadness. It was almost as if his nature had determined the way in which I should mourn him.

To our amazement, Fluffy continued to totter through life, but a few months later we lost another beloved animal. This time literally.

Bruno had calmed down considerably since we moved into The Greenhouse but occasionally when Dave and I weren't around, he'd sneak off down to the beach on his own. We knew he was doing it because he'd come back sopping wet and covered in sea sand.

Early one Sunday morning during the school holidays, I awoke to find him missing. But by the time I had showered and dressed, he was back. Shortly afterwards, Dave called me to help him with a dog in the surgery.

On my way out the front door I paused, looking at Bruno lying on the passage floor.

'Maybe I should close Bruno in the spare room while we're busy,' I suggested.

'I'll only need you for a minute while I inject the dog,' Dave said and so I followed him out of the door.

When I got back to the house five minutes later, Bruno was gone. Taking Beau with me, I hurried down to the beach. It was abuzz with holidaymakers but there was no sign of Bruno.

'Just leave him,' Beau's lips puckered in disapproval. *'If he runs into trouble he'll have only himself to blame.'*

'How can you say that? He's part of our family. We love him.'

'I fail to see how anyone can love an animal that causes chaos wherever it goes,' she said dismissively.

'He doesn't mean to cause chaos. He's just hyperactive.'

'Huh,' she snorted. *'There are those among us who would*

describe his behaviour differently.'

'Oh? Such as?'

'Such as pure hooliganism.'

We checked the beach at intervals throughout the morning without any luck and then at lunchtime Ruth phoned. She had tried to contact us earlier but there had been no reply.

That morning, while fishing on the rocks, she had glanced up to see a dog that looked like Bruno jump into the back of a bakkie with a group of children. Unfortunately she had been too far away to take the registration number.

We placed an advertisement in the local newspaper, although we suspected that the people who had taken him were from out of town. We hoped that if they ever returned for another holiday, he would find his way back to us.

When school holidays came around, we'd scan the beach hopefully, but we never saw him again.

'Good riddance,' was Beau's comment. Sometimes she reminded me of Splittie.

'Oh no!' I exclaimed as I lifted the cover from Stewey's cage.

Stewey was hunched on his perch, gazing up at me almost defiantly, as my eyes took in the blood-spattered cage.

'Dave, come quickly, Stewey's bleeding!' I called out.

When Dave examined Stewey, he discovered that he'd plucked the feathers from his inner thigh, tearing at the flesh until the blood flowed.

'I don't think he's lost much blood,' Dave said. 'It looks much worse than it is.'

It certainly did. A little bit of parrot blood goes a long way. Dave did a skin-scraping to check for the presence of mites but under the microscope he could detect no mites at all.

'I don't understand why he's doing this,' he uttered in frustration. 'I thought that allowing him to roam free would sort out this problem.'

It was the first time this had happened since we adopted Stewey, but it wasn't the last.

Stewey would wait until the scab was almost healed and then suddenly one morning we'd find his cage covered in blood again. Worried that the irritation might be caused by dry skin, we kept a spray gun handy and sprayed him with a fine mist of water at intervals throughout the day. Sometimes we'd take him into the bathroom with us when we were having a bath. Dave said the steamy air was an excellent moisturiser.

Weeks would pass without any attempt at self-mutilation and then just as we were lulled into thinking we'd solved the problem, it would occur yet again.

One evening I walked into the kitchen to find Dave sitting at the table, cutting up small scraps of leather.

'What are you doing?' I asked curiously.

'Making lederhosen.'

'What are lederhosen?'

'Leather shorts.'

'Oh. Who are they for?'

'For Stewey.'

'I see.'

'I'm hoping that if we can prevent him from plucking at his inner thigh for a while, we might break the habit.'

'And we'll have to teach him to yodel too.'

'Chrystal,' Dave sighed heavily, 'this is no laughing matter.'

The lederhosen weren't a resounding success. The problem lay in securing them. After trial and error, Dave produced

a pair that were an excellent fit. But they wouldn't stay up. They just slipped down and we'd find Stewey with his lederhosen around his ankles. And expressing himself at length in a string of expletives.

'Gosh, where did he learn to say THAT?' I asked Dave, recalling the refined gentility of the elderly couple he had belonged to.

'Just ignore the swearing, I have to work out a way of getting these pants to stay up.'

Dave tried elasticised braces, but they'd either slip off Stewey's shoulders or he'd gnaw through them, a faraway expression of vicious satisfaction upon his face.

'Well, one thing we know for sure,' I remarked. 'He's not pining for the Alps.' Dave shot me a bleak look.

We were still battling to find a solution to Stewey's problem when a young woman brought in two barn owl chicks.

A tall palm tree on a nearby farm had been blown over during a gale-force wind. Amongst the fronds the farmer's daughter had discovered a nest containing two live chicks and one dead one. We wouldn't have known they were barn owl chicks if the young woman hadn't observed two adults nesting in the tree prior to its demise.

They could've been vultures, with their semi-bald heads and jutting beaks which curved slightly at the tips. Above the beaks two black beady eyes gazed out truculently upon the world. Their bodies resembled dull-white featherpuffs, small enough to fit into the palm of one's hand, and each puff concealed two tiny sets of needle-sharp talons.

'I do think Hiss and Spit could exercise a bit of restraint,' I said one afternoon, holding out my hands for Dave to see. 'After all, we're only trying to help them.'

He stared at the stippled red lacerations. 'You're supposed

to immobilise the legs when handling them.'

'I do. These are bite marks.'

'They don't bite me.'

'Well, they bite *me*. I'll tell you this: when you're working with barn owl chicks, a bird in the hand is not worth two in the bush.'

Initially they had to be handfed with a mixture of minced meat, pronutro and calcium and vitamin powder. After a while, they began eating from a saucer and Dave decided to move them from the loose cage in the hospital to the spare room.

He placed them in a shallow cardboard tray on a table in one corner of the room.

'Shouldn't they be in a cage or a deeper box?' I asked, eyeing the tray doubtfully.

'They don't move around much,' he said. 'They're still very young.'

Dave was right. Hiss and Spit didn't move around much. They moved only to the edge of the table and muted on to our income tax files stacked underneath. It was a while before we discovered this and by the time we did, invoices, receipts and other records were covered in a thick layer of owl droppings.

Ever since we'd opened the practice, I'd lived in fear of a visit from a revenue official coming to inspect our books. Not that we were trying to conceal income. It was just that with the limited time available to us, the paperwork was in a constant state of disorder.

'I wish they'd come this year,' I remarked, as I scraped at a large hardcover book labelled *Repairs and Maintenance*.

'Who?'

'The tax people.'

'Ah.'

After several weeks, when Hiss and Spit were old enough to learn how to fly, we decided to try and reunite them with their parents. It was a long shot but we felt it was worth a try. The two settled down well in the barn at the farm, where the farmer's daughter provided them with meat every day. Before very long, the parents became aware of their presence and to our delight, after a few initial overtures, they were accepted back into the fold.

One morning we awoke to find Fluffy dead in her little padded basket.

For several days we'd been aware that her general condition was deteriorating and we'd discussed euthanasia. Dave pointed out that she was still eating and drinking, although very little, and did not appear to be in any pain and we decided to wait and see.

When I lifted the blanket to offer her a saucer of warm milk, I thought she was sleeping. She had gone very gently into her goodnight, almost as if she'd faded away.

Filling the Gaps

News of Fluffy's passing must have spread rapidly along the grapevine of collective feline consciousness, because within days cats out there knew that there was an opening. There were two applicants.

My mother phoned to say that she was sending us a kitten.

'But Mom, we already have six cats in the house and one in the surgery.'

'You can find it a home.'

She'd heard the kitten mewing very early that morning and eventually traced the sound to the middle of the overgrown hedge surrounding her property.

'Someone must have put it there,' she said. 'It's too tiny to have found its way there on its own.' She arranged for a friend to bring it to us.

The kitten arrived in a shoebox and Nic took one delighted look at it and named it 'Scratchit John'. Nic's second name was John, as was Dave's and Bill's, and my father's first name had been John.

'It's a family name,' Nic informed us proudly and Dave and I realised that this kitten wasn't going anywhere.

He was a tiny scrap of a thing, mainly white with a few

splotches of black scattered haphazardly across his body. One splotch had landed just above his right eye, giving him a slightly rakish look, as if he was wearing a beret or a displaced eyepatch. Later, when his personality became more apparent, we decided to stick with the eyepatch theory.

The second applicant was a large colour-point male. He arrived a day after Scratchit John in the arms of a client whose house bordered a nature reserve.

'He appears to be living in the reserve,' said Mr Kent. 'I've been feeding him for about four weeks now, but a few days ago I noticed that he was having difficulty urinating.' When Dave examined the cat he discovered that its urethra was partially blocked by crystals, preventing the easy flow of urine. This had resulted in a severe bladder infection and Dave explained that the cat would need a course of antibiotics and would have to be fed a special diet. Mr Kent wasn't keen.

'Look, Doc,' he said, 'it's not as if it's my cat. Wouldn't it be kinder to put it down?'

'Kinder to whom?' I asked cynically, when Dave told me this.

We decided to keep the cat in the surgery until his urinary problem had cleared and we could find him a home. He was magnificent, with his long cream-coloured coat and chocolate-brown points. Despite his large frame, he was fairly thin and a flap of loose skin hanging from his undercarriage was an indication that he'd been more rotund at some stage in the past.

We discovered that although he loved rubbing up against people, he did not enjoy being picked up and held. He'd struggle and kick frantically until you put him down again. Which was rather quickly because he was a very strong cat.

Within three weeks the loose flap of skin all but disappeared as he waded through one dish of food after another. His policy regarding food was simple. If it's edible – eat it. We named him 'Portly'.

'That cat is overeating,' Dave observed one evening. 'Look at him . . . he's like a vacuum cleaner.' We stared at Portly, who was crouched on a table in the hospital, his face buried in a bowl.

'Obesity will just exacerbate his bladder problem,' Dave said sternly. 'We'll have to limit him to one meal per day.'

We adhered strictly to this instruction. I gave him one meal a day. Dave gave him one meal a day. And Johannes gave him one meal a day.

'Who is that for?' Dave asked, coming up behind me as I spooned catfood into a bowl.

'It's for Portly.'

'But I fed him not fifteen minutes ago!'

'Really? But he said . . .' I glanced at Portly who had stopped banging his knife and fork on the table and was staring fixedly at a blemish in the novilon.

'Just look at him,' Dave shook his head. 'He's a complete con-artist. He lies around in the waiting room giving shallow little sighs, pretending to be weak and starving and he's so convincing that clients are bringing him their leftovers.'

We realised that in order to limit Portly's intake, we'd have to move him into the house. At least that would eliminate the tubs of chicken livers, slivers of roast lamb and nuggets of sweet-and-sour pork being presented to him on a daily basis.

But before we could actually implement this plan, a very interesting incident occurred.

On a Saturday morning I was doing reception duty when I heard a female voice exclaim, 'MARCUS AURELIUS!' I looked up to see a well-dressed, middle-aged woman standing in the doorway of the waiting room. I recognised her as Mrs Hatton, a client who had been to see Dave before with her dog. But who was Marcus Aurelius?

'Ummm, I'm not quite sure . . .'

'The cat,' she pointed to the shelf behind me where Portly was reclining full-length, trying to pass the time until his next meal.

'His name is Portly.'

'No, it's Marcus Aurelius. I'd know him anywhere.'

Slightly at a loss, I stared at her.

'Look,' she said, joining me behind the counter, 'here's the scar on his leg where he was bitten by the fox terrier. They were fighting over a bone,' she added. As she said 'bone', Portly's eyes flicked open and he gazed around hopefully. I imagined that fighting a dog over a bone could well be the type of activity he would indulge in.

'Did he have any other distinguishing marks?'

'He had a burn mark under his right front paw from the time he attempted to remove a piece of fish from a sizzling pan.'

I lifted Portly's right front paw and there it was. An old pink scar across his pads.

Portly, alias Marcus Aurelius, had lived with Mrs Hatton for about a year. She'd adopted him when his owners emigrated to Canada. Unfortunately, after a few months he started urinating on their furniture.

It started in a small way, a little wet spot here, a little wet spot there. After a while the little wet spots became little puddles. Then one day Mr Hatton sank down into his favourite armchair to watch the cricket on TV, only to discover after a few seconds that he was sitting in a pool of cat urine. After the fourth such incident he delivered an ultimatum.

A family in Cougadorp, twenty kilometres away, offered

to take Marcus Aurelius, but a few days after he went to them, they phoned Mrs Hatton to report that he was missing.

Taking into account the four weeks he had spent in the vicinity of Mr Kent's home, we calculated that it had taken him two weeks to walk twenty kilometres.

'He was only about one kilometre from home,' I said to Dave. 'I wonder why he stopped?'

'Perhaps he was so starved that when Mr Kent fed him he decided to stick around for a while. Either that or he'd become temporarily disorientated. Maybe he'd been chased by dogs or wildcats in the reserve.'

Dave explained to Mrs Hatton that by urinating on the furniture, Marcus Aurelius had been trying to tell her that something was amiss. But she was reluctant to take him back. She said they'd only just managed to rid the house of the smell of cat urine and her husband would hit the roof if she returned with the culprit.

Portly had shown no sign of trying to wander away from us and after talking about it we decided to keep him. He had already changed owners three times and we felt that was enough for any animal to cope with.

When we put this to him, he said that he was all right with it, as long as the requisite five meals per day were provided. We beat him down to three.

'Call this a meal!' he protested indignantly a few days later, as he gazed down at a bowl containing four green peas.

'It's not your main meal but it's food, therefore it qualifies as a meal.'

'But I don't even like peas!' he moaned, staring at the bowl in dismay. *'And there are only FOUR!'*

'Well, if you don't intend eating them it doesn't really matter how many there are, does it?'

'But . . .'

Filling the Gaps

'In fact you should consider yourself fortunate. I could've given you a WHOLE BOWL of something you didn't like. Think of that.' When I left the kitchen he was sucking mournfully at a single green pea.

We had to keep a close eye on him where food was concerned. Overweight was one of the factors that could lead to a blocked urethra in a castrated male cat. It was a potentially dangerous condition that could result in kidney failure, if not detected quickly. If treatment and a special diet did not control the problem, then surgery was the next step.

Portly and Scratchit John were still settling in when we acquired another dog. The canine population was somewhat behind the feline, when it came to spreading the news.

A few months earlier one of the library members, a Mrs Carling, had popped in with a bundle of books under one arm and a Pekingese under the other.

'What a delightful dog!' I exclaimed and immediately its mouth lolled open, as if it was laughing and two bright bulging eyes glowed in the squashed-up gremlin face.

'He's a gift from our daughter. She and her husband bought him as a pup about eighteen months ago.'

'How could they bear to part with him?'

'They live in a flat and they said it wasn't really working out.'

'Oh? I would've thought he'd be the ideal dog for a flat.'

His name was Cubby and as Mrs Carling left I called out jokingly: 'If you ever get tired of him, you know where to bring him.'

And a few months later that's exactly what she did. She telephoned me at the library and asked if I was still interested in having Cubby.

'Why would you want to give him away?' I asked,

surprised.

'It's not really working out because we go away quite often,' she explained.

'But Chrystal, we already have four dogs,' Dave objected when I told him.

'I know that, but we used to have five before Bruno went missing, and I did say that if she ever wanted to give him away she must bring him to me.'

'You said it jokingly.'

'I know, I know. But he's such a delightful dog.'

Mr Carling dropped Cubby off at the practice on a Saturday morning and when consulting was over, I carried him into the house. He yapped and wriggled excitedly when he saw the other dogs. They snuffed each other thoroughly and when the introductions were finally over, Cubby bounced over to a chair and lifted his leg.

'Oh no, don't do that,' I called out, but it was too late and a stream of urine trickled down the chair leg on to the floor. By the time I returned with a cloth, he was busy on his third chair.

I couldn't keep up with him. He was like 'Quickdraw McGraw'. He marked the sitting room in seventeen places before moving on to our bedroom. Nic assessed the situation at a glance and promptly slammed his bedroom doors shut and kept them closed for the rest of that day. And the next.

'He's not marking MY territory,' he said firmly.

After our bedroom, Cubby proceeded into the garden. He was very thorough. No bush was left untouched.

'Where does he store all the urine?' I asked Dave. 'After all he's only a little dog.'

'He certainly is delightful,' Dave remarked that evening, as we watched Cubby attempting to copulate with the leg of a small occasional table.

'You'll have to castrate him as soon as possible. His hormones are on the rampage. No wonder they said it wasn't working out.'

'I'll try and fit him in next week.'

'What about tomorrow?'

'Tomorrow's Sunday. I'm not doing a castration on a Sunday.'

'Well, Monday then. At the latest.'

'Nic, look at that! Isn't it beautiful?'

I stepped back to gaze admiringly at the Christmas tree which was propped up in a bucket in the middle of the sitting room. The string of bright festive lights draped over the branches flashed on and off, illuminating the sparkling silver and gold decorations and the gleaming red swathes of tinsel.

'Let's move it into the corner and find some stones to fill the bucket.'

As I spoke, the telephone rang and I hurried into the darkened passage to answer it. My foot slammed into a solid object and I tripped, falling forward over Jade who was sprawled out on the floor, fast asleep. Jerked from her slumber, she lurched to her feet, catapulting me into the air. As I hit the wall, I grabbed desperately at the telephone shelf. The telephone went flying as Jade shot from the passage into the sitting room and I heard a muffled 'clunk', followed by a rustling sound.

'MOM!' Nic shrieked in dismay.

Righting myself, I staggered into the sitting room, just in time to see Jade, the string of brightly flashing lights looped around her neck, hurtle out through the sliding doors

dragging the Christmas tree behind her.

'JADE,' I yelled. 'STOP!' There was a 'plop' as the plug was ripped from the wall and the lights stopped flashing.

I had decided that this Christmas would be special. It was our very first Christmas in our own house and to celebrate, I'd gone out and bought a real Christmas tree, a selection of shiny decorations, streams of red glossy tinsel and a set of lights.

We hadn't had our own tree since Nic was born. We'd always had to vacate the sea-house over Christmas and when we moved into the cottage, the sitting room was too small to accommodate a tree. Dodo and Bill had a small artificial tree the size of a potplant but I'd longed to have a proper tree for Nic. One that would fill the house with the smell of pine and shed its needles in the New Year, so that you knew Christmas was finally over.

We caught up with Jade at the bottom of the steps leading into the garden. When the lights came on again, the tree was squatting safely atop a wooden chest. In a bucket filled to the brim with heavy bricks.

The lights never really made a full recovery. They'd flash erratically for a while, then flicker weakly and go out, as if they were tired. We'd have to shake the tree violently to get them going again.

At the Drop of a Hat

'WHO LET THE CAT OUT OF THE BAG?'

The indignant yell issued from Nic's room, down the passage and around the corner into the kitchen, where I was washing dishes at the sink. I paused for a moment, listening.

'Mo omm . . . Mo om.'

'MOM!' I jumped.

'Yes, Nic?'

'I've been calling you. Why didn't you answer?'

'Er . . .'

'Did you let Scratchit John out of the bag?' he demanded imperiously.

'Yes.'

'But WHY? I was keeping him there while I had a swim.'

'Nic, cats don't like being in bags. It's an accepted historical fact.'

'Scratchit John does. He purrs when I put him in.'

'He doesn't purr when you let him out. He gets stuck into the other animals and they're petrified of him.'

'Beau isn't.'

'Beau's different. Remember what happened to Jade last week, when you let him out of the cupboard.'

'No?'

'He clawed into her back and when I rushed to see what the commotion was about, he was shouting, *Ride 'em, cowboy.*'

'I'm sure Jade didn't mind.'

'The whites of her eyes were showing and she ran the door right off the TV cabinet.'

'But, Mom, she's always breaking things.'

'Exactly! She doesn't need to be terrorised into breaking more.'

'I'm sorry, it was unfortunate.'

'It was unnecessary.'

Scratchit John loved Nic with all his heart and soul. Without a murmur of protest, he would play the role of the imprisoned princess, waiting to be rescued from her castle – a cardboard box. Or the Count of Monte Cristo, languishing in his underground dungeon – a drawer. Dressed in a baby's bonnet and matinée jacket, he'd allow himself to be pushed around in a pram.

But woe betide the casual onlooker when the bonnet came off and the matinée jacket hit the fan. One of his favourite pastimes involved dropping down from a height on to the back of some unsuspecting dog or cat. Dave and I had started referring to him 'The Assassin'.

Since the advent of Scratchit John, Pookie had become a fugitive who slunk out into the garden at cockcrow, only returning at night when he was tucked up safely under Nic's duvet. All our efforts to persuade her to stand her ground proved fruitless. She said having an animal claw your back when you least expected it was not conducive to mental health. Her nerves were shot, she said.

Seafood maintained her usual low profile and managed to avoid him most of the time, but poor old Gobby became a regular victim. He was a sitting duck on top of that rubbish bin lid.

'What've I done to him?' he whined, having been knocked off the lid for the fifth successive time that morning.

'You've done nothing. It's just youthful exuberance.'

'I keep myself to myself, I'm not doing any harm.'

'Of course not, we know that,' I murmured reassuringly, dusting him off. 'Hopefully, it's just a phase.'

Portly handled the assaults by pretending to be an inanimate object and before long Scratchit John lost interest. Obviously without the screaming and writhing it wasn't much fun. Carrots cancelled his gun catalogue subscription and began saving for the real thing. *'After all, you can't shoot anyone with a catalogue,'* he explained.

Arrow, Jade, Flenny and Cubby were prime targets, always good for an exhilarating bareback ride. Only Beau and Pushcat managed to resist the onslaughts. Pushcat kept her hockey stick to hand at all times and Beau had perfected the silent snarl.

Without making a sound she'd lift her lips and bare her powerful canines, while her eyes flashed molten threats at Scratchit John. Unfortunately, before long I discovered that she was using this tactic on Nic's friends.

'AUNTIE CHRYSTAL . . . AUNTIE CHRYSTAL!' They'd come running to me, screeching in terror. 'SAVE US!'

'From what . . . from what?' I'd ask, alarmed.

'THE WOLF! It wants to eat us!'

'What wolf?'

'THAT ONE!' pointing to Beau, who'd gaze back at me blandly.

'But she's not doing anything.'

'She tried to eat us!'

'Don't be silly, it must be your imagination.'

After several such incidents I became suspicious.

'Beau?'

'*Yes?*'

'Are you trying to eat Nic's friends?'

'*Absolutely not. I just show them my teeth and click them a few times.*'

'But they're Nic's friends.'

'*They hurt him.*'

'They're only children, it's playful wrestling.'

'*They're dangerous,*' she said darkly. '*They hurt him and I'm not allowing it.*'

I sighed. Basically, Beau regarded any person who did not actually reside in our home as a potential enemy. To her way of thinking, there was a reason for them not living with us, and that was because they weren't to be trusted. If a visitor attempted to befriend her she would view that individual with the deepest suspicion, convinced that they were up to no good. And whereas she used the silent approach on boisterous children and animals, when it came to adults she'd pull out all the stops.

She'd launch herself at them, barking frenziedly, stiff forelegs drumming on the floor, teeth slavering with all the savagery of a wild animal in attack mode. I was pretty sure she had no intention of biting them. But they didn't know that.

And she hated hats with a passion.

She associated them with the dregs of society, murderers, rapists, thieves and the like. Nothing I could say would change this rigid opinion.

'You cannot go through life regarding people who wear hats as desperate criminals.'

'*They're hiding something.*'

'They're hiding their heads from the sun. And some people wear hats to church. Look at Mrs Kowalski, she wears a hat.'

Beau shot me a sardonic look, as if I'd just proved her point.

There was nothing mysterious about Beau's hatred of headgear. We knew where it originated. The day, the hour, and even the minute.

Mr Howell, one of Dave's clients, was a dog-training instructor from the Northern Cape who specialised in attack training. Every year he and his wife spent a month in Dolphin Bay on holiday. Their three Rottweilers always accompanied them and they'd bring the dogs in for their annual check-ups and vaccinations. Over the years Dave and Mr Howell had had long discussions about the methods used in attack training and eventually one day Mr Howell suggested a demonstration, using Beau and Jade.

We arranged to meet at an open field on a Sunday morning and when we arrived with the two dogs, Mr Howell was already waiting, dressed in a thickly padded protective suit and wearing a khaki-coloured baseball cap.

'Why is he wearing a padded suit?' I asked.

'Because this is an attack training demonstration.'

'Dave, I'm not sure this is such a good idea.'

'I think it'll be very interesting. He's going to demonstrate how one would assess a dog as a suitable candidate for attack training.'

Dave strolled over to Mr Howell and a few minutes later, he returned.

'We're going to work with Jade first,' he said. 'You and Beau can wait here at the bakkie.'

Beau and I watched as Dave put Jade on-lead and began walking across the field towards Mr Howell. As they drew level with him, he suddenly produced a thick stick from behind his back and lunged at Dave.

Two things happened simultaneously. Jade yelped and

flinched away, looking confused, and at my side Beau started growling. Deeeep in her throat. When Mr Howell repeated the attempt, Beau's growling intensified, and by the third try I was having difficulty in restraining her.

Jade, on the other hand, had decided to ignore the stick. She didn't understand what this man was up to with his stick. Obviously he had no intention of throwing it for her to fetch. So she just ignored it. Despite the fact that physically she was a prime specimen of the Dobermann breed, she did not appear to have a natural aggression. I was pleased. Being the inconvenient dog she was, I knew that if ever she attacked anyone, it would be the wrong person. Probably some innocent fending off a mugger.

But at my side the Pandora's Box was well and truly open. Beau wagged her tail as Dave and Jade approached. She licked Jade's face as if to comfort her, but when her gaze shifted past Jade to Mr Howell, her expression hardened.

'He says don't keep her on a tight lead, he wants her to have the leeway to react,' Dave told me.

'Dave, Beau is going to bite him.'

'She can't hurt him, he's wearing the suit.'

'But . . .'

'Chrystal, the whole point of the exercise is to see if she would attack, given the right circumstances.'

Sighing heavily, I set off across the field with Beau. She stalked rather than walked, her eyes narrowed to slits as she locked her gaze on Mr Howell. On her back a ridge of glinting hair bristled as if electrified. When we were a few metres away from him a rumble started in her chest, working its way upwards, sifting through her canines in a sinister snarl. Even the lead in my hand seemed to vibrate.

Mr Howell's stick-hand was still behind his back when she attacked. She leapt for his throat and, taken by surprise and momentarily off-balance, he tumbled backwards, falling to the ground. As he fell, he threw his free arm across his face and throat and Beau sank her teeth into it, ripping viciously at the padding.

'BEAU!' I shouted, heaving at the lead. For a few desperate seconds I thought she wasn't going to obey, but with one final wrench at the padded arm, she released it and turned to me.

'Come, Beau, come,' I said, backing away as Dave ran up and helped Mr Howell to his feet. Beau and I returned to the bakkie and waited for Dave.

'Well, that sorted him out,' she snorted with grim satisfaction.

'It was overkill.'

'Him and his cap and his nasty shifty eyes.'

'There's nothing wrong with his eyes. They're perfectly normal.'

'They're shifty,' she stated flatly. *'And he was trying to hide them under the cap.'*

Hidden Treasures

I paused at the bottom of the steps, watching the dogs streak across the beach towards the water. Apart from their tracks, the sand had been swept smooth by an early afternoon wind. The wind had subsided now and as I stood facing the sea, the sun was setting behind me.

Shadows cast by houses bordering the dunes crept across the sand towards the waterline like sinister fingers reaching out to steal the light. On the horizon, sea and sky merged in misty layers of pink, pale purple and frosted blue. It was hard to see where one ended and the other began. The air was crisp and I inhaled, drawing it deep into my lungs. As I exhaled slowly, I felt the stress seeping away.

Things had started to go wrong that morning when I unlocked the library door, almost as if I'd unlocked the day's potential for chaos. Or perhaps chaos was too strong a word; maybe just a touch of mayhem.

As I stepped inside the library, a medium-sized brown dog which had been sitting on the steps bounded in after me. It rushed over to one of the padded pouffes in the children's section and began gnawing at a corner.

'No, don't do that,' I cried. 'That's naughty. Come here.'

It gambolled over to me, wagging its tail happily. I wondered whose dog it was. Maybe it belonged to holiday people? Being a coastal town, Dolphin Bay saw a constant stream of new faces coming and going. Families often brought their dogs on holiday with them and sometimes these dogs would become disorientated in the unfamiliar surroundings and wander off.

When I opened the door to let it out, it didn't want to leave.

'OK, you can stay as long as you behave,' I said sternly. Picking up a stack of books, I began shelving.

When I returned for the second stack, the dog was stretched out on the floor in the non-fiction section chewing at the bottom row of books.

'That's it. Now you'll have to leave.'

The dog dug its paws into the carpet, refusing to budge, and in the end I had no option but to carry it to the door. I dumped it on the steps and closed the door quickly before it could come back inside. By this time I was sweating slightly as the dog was quite a weight. Returning to the shelves, I ignored the frantic whining and scratching outside.

One hour later it was time to open to the public. As I opened the door the dog shot back inside.

'GET OUT!' I yelled and a gentleman who had been waiting on the steps, teetered backwards and almost fell.

'I'm so sorry,' I apologised. 'I was addressing the dog.'

He stared at me warily and edged over to the counter.

'I'll be with you in a minute,' I told him. 'I need to remove that dog before it damages more books.'

Once more, the dog stubbornly refused to cooperate. Dragging it to the door, I gave it a shove with my foot.

'Now STAY OUT, you miserable animal!' I hissed, beginning to feel slightly harassed.

I went back behind the counter, but as the gentleman handed me his books I saw the dog nip into the reading room behind him.

'OH DAMN!' I exclaimed.

The man jumped nervously.

'It's the dog,' I explained. 'It's back inside.'

He glanced behind him. There wasn't a dog in sight.

'It's in the reading room,' I said feeling foolish.

Without saying a word, he took his cards from me and left.

I spent the next hour hauling the dog out of every corner of the library.

I was at a loss to know what to do. If I closed the front door, the public would think the library was closed. If only it wasn't such a perfect day, I thought, I could've placed the *'Closed on account of the weather'* notice on the door. Unfortunately the sky was a radiant blue and there wasn't a cloud in sight.

An SPCA facility for the Dolphin Bay area was still in the planning stage and eventually, in desperation, I telephoned Dave. He offered to keep the dog in a cage in the hospital until we could trace its owners and he sent Johannes over to collect it.

By the time Johannes drove off, I was way behind schedule. I had planned an Easter egg treasure hunt for the children that afternoon and still had to hide the eggs and come up with several clues.

At one o'clock when it was time to close for lunch, the eggs were in place, but I was still five clues short. I decided to complete the clues at home and after locking up hurriedly I sped off in the Beetle. On that day the library reopened at three o'clock and two hours would be more than enough time, I hoped.

'The library ghost is at his post . . . and where he sits to read at night . . . there you'll find me . . . out of sight.' With a sigh of relief, I penned the final clue and, glancing at my watch, I saw that it was a quarter to three.

As I pulled into the library parking lot, a crowd of children and adults were milling around. When I saw the adults my heart sank. When I'd advertised the treasure hunt in the local newspaper, I'd diplomatically suggested that adults would be wise to avoid the library on that particular afternoon.

I threaded my way through the crowd and as I approached the front door I saw to my amazement an elderly gentleman leaning from one of the windows, his elbows resting on the sill. How on earth had he managed to get inside?

I had locked him in. When I closed up at one o'clock he'd been sitting in the reading room, engrossed in a magazine. Apparently it was a while before he discovered that he was alone. He said he'd read all the magazines. From cover to cover.

Several adults were queuing to return their books and after settling the children down in their section with a few games, I began taking in books. The children were excited and before long the building resounded to the babble of shrill voices.

'I thought libraries were supposed to be quiet places,' one woman remarked snidely as I took her books from her.

'If you'd read the newspaper you'd know you're not supposed to be here,' I said coldly.

She drew back, looking offended, and as I handed her her cards, a red-haired woman carrying a cardboard box stepped up to the counter. I'd seen her before. She'd recently moved into the house next door to the library and although we'd never been introduced, I'd heard that she was a very talented sculptor.

I noticed that blood was welling from a nasty cut on her chin.

'A French couple have just knocked on my door and handed me this,' she said expressionlessly as she placed the box on the counter. I stared at the box.

'It's a penguin.'

'Oh.'

The couple, communicating in a combination of broken English and sign language, had explained that the lady at the municipal offices had instructed them to bring the penguin to her. When she protested that she knew nothing about penguins, they said '*Merci beaucoup*', placed the box on the ground and left.

Apparently when she opened the box to check its contents, the penguin had lunged at her, catching her on the chin with its beak.

I took the box from the counter and carried it to the bathroom, trailed by a herd of noisy children.

'Is it the treasure, Miss?' they shrilled. 'Is it the treasure?'

'It's not the treasure hunt treasure, but it's the real treasure,' I told them.

The light was almost gone, the sun a distant memory behind the hills, when I called to the dogs and turned to retrace my steps. The tide was pushing in strongly, sending small waves to foray around my bare feet, causing them to sink more deeply into the waterlogged sand with each step.

Higher up the beach a group of seagulls was squabbling over a dead shark, and as they jostled for position and hurled insults at each other, I was reminded of the children that afternoon.

They were so clever. Before I'd even finished reading out the first clue, they were off. They swarmed down passageways and between shelves, baying at the scent. The triumphant yells which heralded success quickly changed to pained yelps, as they vied for possession of the eggs. Within minutes, the few adults who had been so determined to use the library that afternoon, had left hurriedly.

I mounted the wooden steps and at the top I paused to brush the sea sand from my feet, feeling tranquil and relaxed. As if the sea had absorbed my stress, soaking it up and dispersing it into watery green depths, until it no longer existed.

'If I didn't know better, I'd swear this was feline babesiosis,' Dave muttered, hunched over the microscope. Feline babesiosis was biliary or tick-bite fever in cats.

'Why can't it be feline babesiosis?'

'Because I'm looking at Treasure's bloodsmear.'

'Oh.'

The penguin which had arrived on the day of the treasure hunt was an adult. Although fairly aggressive, it was thin and weak and we were a bit puzzled by this. There was no obvious reason that we could see for its condition. It wasn't oiled or injured and did not appear to be post-moult. When a penguin emerges from a moult, its white plumage is a clean radiant white. Treasure's white feathers were grubby, as if they'd been around for a while.

Its mucous membranes were paper-white and Dave dewormed it, but despite this, over the next few days the anaemia remain unchanged and it became even weaker. On the fourth day he took a bloodsmear to check for avian malaria, although the symptoms weren't typical.

When he checked the smear under the microscope, there was no sign of avian malaria, but the red blood cells were riddled with parasites which closely resembled those of feline babesiosis.

I stared at Dave. 'But surely penguins don't get biliary?'

Biliary in dogs and cats along the Eastern Cape coast was rife – but biliary in penguins?

'Not that I know of,' Dave shrugged. 'But that's what the parasites in these red blood cells look like. And it's not the first time I've seen something like this in a penguin smear.'

Dave phoned an avian specialist at Onderstepoort, the veterinary faculty in Pretoria. Professor Duggan was very interested and said that a few years before, an anatomist involved in research at one of the universities had detected Babesia parasites in a penguin's blood. He asked Dave to send him a bloodsmear and suggested that in the mean time he start treatment with antiprotozoals and antibiotics.

Over the next two days Treasure's condition deteriorated even further, but Dave persevered. He was used to seeing a similar pattern in cats, when treatment was initiated. As the Babesia parasites were killed off by the antiprotozoals, the red blood cells harbouring them usually died as well, exacerbating the anaemia. The crucial objective was to keep the patient alive while its bone marrow produced new red blood cells.

After five days, Treasure's mucous membranes took on a pink tinge and he began swallowing small pieces of fish. Two days later he took a whole fish.

Professor Duggan confirmed the diagnosis and once

Dave knew what to look for, he began picking up more cases. He alerted vets dealing with penguins at SANCCOB in Cape Town and the Oceanarium in Port Elizabeth and before long they were picking up cases too.

Dave decided that from then on he would take a blood-smear from each penguin upon admission. Where the results were positive he started treatment immediately. Within a few months, we noticed an improvement in the survival rate of penguins we were handling and we realised that some of the previously unexplained deaths could be attributed to biliary.

Laying it on thick

At the beginning of October, Dave decided that it was time for him and Nic to pay a visit to Roger and Gail and their two children, Thomas and Emma, in Cape Town. Nic would be starting school the following year and from then on getting away would be limited to school holidays which were usually busy times in the surgery. October was a quiet month and an ideal time for Dave to take a break. Unfortunately, I'd used up all my leave and wouldn't be able to go with them. They planned to leave early on a Wednesday morning.

At lunchtime on the Tuesday I walked into our bedroom to find Stewey lying on his back on the facebrick floor, his toes curled up, his eyes shut. He appeared to be unconscious.

Despite the fact that my knowledge of birds was still fairly limited, even I knew that this was not a good sign. A parrot lying on its back with its feet in the air has about the same status as a goldfish floating belly-up in a bowl.

'Stewey!' I cried. 'What's happened to you?'

As I lifted him, his eyes fluttered open and he lay in my hands, gazing up at me blankly.

'I think he's suffered a stroke,' Dave said as he examined him.

'Will he live?'

'It all depends.'

Dave explained that the first few hours after a stroke are crucial. Movement regained in those hours was a significant indication of whether or not there would be a full recovery.

When I returned from the library late that afternoon, Dave was still busy consulting. With Stewey in his jacket pocket.

'He can stand now but he can't walk yet,' Dave told me.

'Why is he in your pocket?'

'Because when I'm not watching him, he tries to bite at his left wing.'

Stewey's left wing was hanging as a result of the stroke, but apart from that and the general weakness in his legs, Dave reported that his condition was stable.

'I think he's going to be OK, but you'll have to do some physiotherapy with him.'

'Me?'

'Yes. We can't take him with us to Cape Town.'

'I suppose not.'

That night, Stewey slept on Dave's chest, loosely wrapped in a small hand towel. When we awoke at five o'clock the next morning, we were relieved to see that he'd made no attempt to mutilate his wing during the night.

'He'll be fine now,' Dave said. 'He's eating and drinking and you'll just have to exercise his wing and legs every two hours or so.'

'I'll have to take him to work with me.'

'Use the small picnic basket. It's big enough for a hot water bottle and he needs to be kept fairly warm.'

By seven o'clock the bakkie was packed and Dave and Nic were ready to set off. Feeling a bit forlorn, I stood on the pavement waving as they disappeared around the corner.

When I walked back into the bedroom to get ready for

Laying it on thick

work, I discovered that Stewey had managed to wriggle out of the hand towel and was busy gnawing at his left wing, which was already bleeding in several places.

'That's very naughty of you!' I exclaimed. Grabbing the towel, I wrapped him up again. But ten minutes later when I emerged from the bathroom, he was at it again.

'What am I going to do with you?' I sighed.

When I was ready to leave I opened the door of the Beetle and placed the picnic basket on the passenger seat. As I climbed in behind the wheel I glanced into the basket, where Stewey lay glaring up at me resentfully. A crêpe bandage was wound firmly around his body from his neck to his tail.

'Now you look just like an Egyptian mummy,' I smirked.

That evening Dave phoned to tell me that he and Nic had arrived safely. The next morning I awoke to grey skies and pouring rain and when I returned from work that afternoon, all the dogs were sneezing. Every last one of them.

'Please don't get sick now,' I said, gazing at them in alarm. The words weren't cold on my lips, when Flenny burst into a paroxysm of coughing. I examined her throat and found that it was very red.

'Give her a dose of cough mixture,' Dave advised when I phoned him. 'If she's not better by tomorrow afternoon, you'll have to start her on a course of antibiotics.'

We hadn't realised it at the time, but the stroke had affected Stewey's ability to speak. For three days after the stroke he never said a word. Then on the fourth day, as he lay in his basket in the library, staring up at the ceiling, he regained his powers of speech.

'SON OF A BI . . .' he began truculently and I coughed loudly in an attempt to drown out the last word.

'What is he saying?' asked an elderly lady, who was waiting at the counter.

Laying it on thick

'I'm not sure.'

His physiotherapy was causing quite a stir at the library, but strangely enough, not amongst the children. They looked on casually, as if seeing a librarian perform physiotherapy on a parrot was an everyday occurrence in their lives. It was the adults who could barely contain their curiosity.

'Just pop your books on to the counter, I'll see to them in a minute,' I'd call out from the table where Stewey lay on his back as I pedalled his little legs. A few seconds of silence would follow and then . . .

'What is it?'

'A parrot.'

'What are you doing to it?'

'I'm giving it physiotherapy.'

'Why?'

'It had a stroke.'

'I didn't know parrots could have strokes.'

'Neither did I.'

'Are you sure it's a stroke?'

'My husband said it was.'

'Have you had it to a vet?'

'Yes.'

'What did he say?'

'The same as my husband.'

By Friday, Flenny's coughing hadn't improved and when Cubby started coughing too I put them both on to antibiotics. Then on Saturday morning I noticed that Gobby was limping badly. It was an old war wound, he said, and in cold rainy weather it gave him gyp.

'Give him a dose of anti-inflammatory syrup,' Dave suggested, when I finally managed to get hold of him on the phone.

'My teeth are aching,' Carrots offered hopefully, as he

watched Gobby suck the last drops of syrup from his two exposed canines with every evidence of enjoyment.

'It's caramel-flavoured. You don't like caramel.'

'Doesn't it come in any other flavour?'

'I'm afraid not. Just the caramel.'

'Oh.'

'If your teeth are really bad, I could always take you to the dentist for an injection.'

'NO! They're fine now actually . . . I think it was just a passing twinge.'

On Monday when I emerged from the library at lunchtime, the Beetle refused to start. When I turned the key in the ignition, the engine gave a sullen whine and then spluttered into silence. Carrying Stewey in his basket, I hurried back inside through the driving rain to phone Bill. He drove down to take me home and offered to ferry me back and forth each day, until I could find a mechanic to come and look at the vehicle. It was very kind of him, as there was considerable inconvenience involved.

On Tuesday morning I noticed that Stewey had diarrhoea. Reluctant to phone Dave yet again, that afternoon I telephoned a colleague of his in Cougadorp. I knew that diarrhoea in parrots could result in mortality if left untreated.

Frank gave me the names and dosages of a few remedies and fortunately when I checked the dispensary I found that we had one of them in stock.

'You'll have to dose him directly into his crop,' Frank told me.

Bound up as he was in his crêpe bandage, Stewey couldn't put up much of a struggle, but as I inserted the tube into his throat, he managed to get out a few choice words. Somewhat muffled but still recognisable.

'Language, language,' I remonstrated gently.

Laying it on thick

On Wednesday morning I woke up feeling exhausted and wondered when Dave and Nic were coming home. Dave had been rather vague when I asked him. He said they would play it by ear. Anyway, thank God it was Wednesday. The library was closed on Wednesday afternoons and I really felt the need to unwind.

When Bill dropped me off at home I had a leisurely lunch and then went to lie down. At four o'clock I awoke feeling refreshed and decided to take Beau, Jade and Arrow to the beach. Cubby and Flenny were still coughing slightly and I was reluctant to expose them to the icy wind. Usually I avoided taking Jade to the beach because she behaved so badly when allowed off-lead. But Dave wasn't there to walk her and if I kept her on-lead she wouldn't be able to race off after seagulls.

On the beach an icy gale-force wind was churning up the sea and mountainous waves were crashing on to the shore. I strolled along the sand, trying to ignore Jade's frantic jerks each time she spotted a seagull. In the distance I spotted two young boys on bodyboards in the heaving surf. As I approached I noticed that one youngster was wearing flippers. The other wasn't and he was being tossed about by the waves. From where I was standing, he didn't seem bothered by this, but I felt a vague sense of unease. A sea as rough as this was no place for children – or most adults, for that matter.

There were no adults in sight, only a group of boys kicking a ball around on the sand. Presumably the two in the surf were part of this group. Perhaps the parents lived in one of the houses overlooking the beach and were monitoring the situation from there. The group on the sand did not appear to be over concerned about the two in the water and I walked on past them and rounded the curve of the bay at the point.

Twenty minutes later I turned for home and when I rounded the point once more, I spotted the two boys. They were still in the water. The group on the beach had disappeared and the only other people in sight were a young couple and a baby further down the beach.

As I drew level with the two boys I paused and watched them. I could see they were trying to make their way in to shore, but while the one wearing flippers was slowly gaining ground, the other was making no headway at all. Despite his bodyboard, or maybe because of it, he was being flung to and fro by the breakers. As I watched he was gradually being swept sideways and further out to sea. To the left of him, a reef of rock appeared and disappeared again amidst the turbulent waters.

Dear God, please don't let this child get into difficulties, I prayed. I'm not a strong enough swimmer for this sea.

Just then, the young boy raised his right arm, waved it frantically in the air and screamed, 'HELLLP . . . HELLLP!'

My mind went blank and for a split second I froze. Then letting go of Jade's lead, I ripped off my sweater and raced towards the water in my pants and T-shirt. As I ran I shouted 'STAY' to Beau and waved frantically at the young couple, trying to attract their attention.

'GET HELP!' I shrieked and pointed to the young boy in the water. My words were sucked into the howling wind and I wasn't sure whether they could hear me.

And then I was in the water. A massive wave broke over me, knocking me off my feet. As I surfaced, my body suddenly slammed into the reef of sharp rock. I grabbed on to the rock and began pulling myself deeper into the sea towards the young boy. His friend had turned back to help him and was holding on to his bodyboard, as they were both washed sideways towards the reef. By the time I reached the point where the reef ended, they were only a few metres away.

Taking a deep breath, I launched myself out into the open sea and as it sucked me towards them, I lunged out and gripped the youngster's upper arm. He let go of his bodyboard and as he did so a huge wave gathered us up and hurled us towards the reef. Out of the corner of my eye, I glimpsed the boy's friend, kicking and paddling madly as he and his bodyboard were carried towards the shore.

As we collided with the reef, I scrabbled desperately with my feet and my free arm, trying to get a grip on the rock before the sea sucked us back again. 'I'm not thirteen yet!' the young boy wailed. I wondered why he was telling me this.

The next wave broke my tenuous hold on the rock, tumbling us over and over, completely out of our depth. I grimly hung on to the young boy's arm and kicked forward, trying to gain as much ground as possible before the wave drew back. Another huge wave surged in and swept us up on to the reef. As my feet brushed against rock, I sank below the surface and hooked my toes into a crevice, trying desperately to anchor the two of us before we were sucked backwards. Another wave boiled in and another and suddenly my feet jolted down on to solid sand and I stumbled and almost fell.

Beau and Arrow were waiting at the water's edge and Beau jumped up at me, frantic with relief. I looked around for the young couple and the baby and spotted them standing in the car park. They waved to me and I waved back.

'Are you all right?' I asked the boy. He nodded, but I noticed that his face was as white as a sheet, his lips blue and trembling. He was obviously in shock and stood hunched over, shivering uncontrollably, his arms clasped around his chest. His friend ran up with a towel and draped it over him and after a mumbled 'thank you' in my direction, he trailed up the beach towards a pile of clothing.

I watched him go, suddenly feeling weak at the knees. There was just one chilling thought in my mind. What if I hadn't been able to save him?

After a while I became aware of the freezing wind slicing through my wet clothes. I walked slowly towards my discarded sweater and pulled it on. I glanced down at my feet and saw that they were cut and bleeding. In the distance I glimpsed Jade tearing across the sand after a seagull. I called to her but she ignored me and I started squelching back along the beach towards home.

Dave and Nic came home on the Friday. In his excitement at seeing them, Stewey promptly shed his crêpe bandage and stood up and walked.

When I awoke on the Saturday morning the sky was clear, the sun was shining and Flenny and Cubby had stopped coughing. Later that morning Gobby announced that his leg was cured. Apparently he gave full credit to Pushcat for her *'laying on of the hands'*. Carrots brought me the news and when he told me, I stared at him thoughtfully.

'Laying on of the hands . . . or laying on of the hockey stick?'

'He said hands.'

'OK.'

Spirit Levels

I had been working at the library for almost three years when I finally accepted that it was haunted.

This acceptance was triggered by Kevin's experience and reinforced by the business with the book, but when I looked back over the previous few years, I knew that the suspicion had been there right from the beginning. However, when the thought first occurred to me, I had dismissed it firmly.

'There will be no ghosts,' I had told myself. 'No ghosts, no spectres, and absolutely NO WRAITHS! Not in this library.'

A few months after I was appointed, the provincial librarian informed me that I'd have to take stock of the books. Apparently stocktaking was done every three years and it was overdue.

After several frustrating days, I was forced to concede that this was not a task that could be undertaken while the library was open to the public. No sooner had I recorded a book as being on the shelf than someone would take it out and at the end of the day, I would record the book as being in the issues. To be absolutely sure that this was the same book, I'd have to go back and check the shelf to confirm that it wasn't there. Doing stocktaking in stages was possible, but it would have to be at times when the library was closed to the public – when books were maintaining their status and not floating around like *Christmas Present* and *Christmas Past*.

When I mentioned to Dodo that I'd have to do the stocktaking at night, she suggested that Nic stay and have supper with them on the nights I had to work late. She said Dave could pop over and fetch him once consulting was over.

So the following afternoon when the last person left at five o'clock, I closed the doors and got stuck in. As I worked, the muffled sounds of passing traffic and pedestrians gradually subsided and a deep silence seemed to settle in the building. Every little noise I made seemed unnaturally loud and I wished I'd brought a radio. As darkness fell outside, the shelves began creaking under the weight of the books. The creaks became more and more enthusiastic and before long they'd progressed into rending groans – the sort of sound you'd expect to hear issuing from a medieval torture chamber. As the rack was cranked tighter and tighter.

I was no scientist, but it was obvious to me that some form of expansion or contraction was taking place here. I wondered why I had never heard the sounds during the day.

When I looked up at eight o'clock it was pitch dark outside and shortly after this the tapping started. *Tap . . . tap . . . tap. Tap . . . tap . . . tap.*

As I ticked off books against catalogue cards, the sound seeped from my subconscious mind into my conscious mind, and after a while I paused, pen in hand, and stood listening.

Tap . . . tap . . . tap. Tap . . . tap . . . tap.

The sounds appeared to be coming from the passageway between the library and the room housing the shell collection. I walked into the passage and waited quietly for the next tap. Nothing but silence. I opened the door to the shell room and switched on the lights. The shells gleamed palely under the fluorescent lights and I could see no possible source of a tapping sound. Shrugging, I switched off the lights and strode back to the shelves. And as I did so, the tapping started again.

Tap . . . tap . . . tap. This time the taps seemed to be coming from the direction of the reading room, but when I entered the reading room the taps ceased abruptly.

Feeling a bit uneasy, I picked up the cards and resumed checking. The tapping didn't start again, but as I worked I became aware of a sensation of being watched. It was as if there was a presence on the periphery of my vision but when I swung my head to look, there was nothing, except books and the open doorway to the reading room.

By nine o'clock I was becoming increasingly edgy and finding it difficult to concentrate and I decided to call it a day.

To my dismay, when I was ready to leave I realised that the light switches for the main library area were situated on the wall of the alcove leading into the passage. This had never been a problem during the day but at night it meant that once I'd switched off the lights, I'd have to make my way in darkness to the front door.

Fighting the temptation to leave the lights on overnight, I walked over to the front door and opened it. Leaving it ajar, I hurried back to the alcove. As my fingers brought the switches down, a frisson of fear rippled across my scalp and the hair rose on the back of my neck. The blackness was total, there was no moonlight at all.

With every goosebump on my arms shrieking 'RUN!' I cautiously shuffled forwards, feeling my way along the shelves. When my flailing hand finally made contact with the door frame, in one swift movement I leapt out on to the steps and slammed the door behind me. With my heart thudding in my chest, I inserted the key in the lock and turned it quickly.

Once the door was locked I felt safe. Which was silly really, I thought, as I walked towards to the Beetle. Because ghosts have never had much truck with doors. To them doors are immaterial.

After this experience I decided to complete the stock-taking over the weekend. During the hours of daylight. And from then on, where humanly possible, I avoided being on my own in the library at night. When the workload was particularly heavy, I'd work on after closing time, always making sure that I left the building before darkness set in. I knew it was silly but I did it anyway.

One evening at twilight, as I prepared to depart leaving several tasks undone, I spoke to myself very severely.

'Now you're being ridiculous,' I said. 'Another hour and you would've finished the reports.'

A small voice murmured in my head: 'In another hour it will be dark.'

'So what? It's not as if you're going to turn into a pumpkin when night falls.'

'It's not pumpkins you're worried about, is it?'

When I was in my third year at the library, the municipality decided to employ a curator to upgrade and maintain the shell collection. Despite the fact that it attracted many visitors, both overseas and local, it was very neglected.

Carol was a petite brunette and she loved shells with a passion. They were her life. She owned an extremely valuable collection herself and her knowledge was extensive. New cabinets were commissioned and once they were installed, Carol informed me that she would be working on the collection at night, when the library and shell room were closed. The shells needed to be cleaned and reclassified, she said, and it was awkward to do this during the day when visitors were wafting in and out.

When she told me this, I stared at her thoughtfully, wondering if I should say anything about what wafted around the library at night. I decided against it. Maybe it was just me.

A few members of my family on my mother's side are fey. They have a sixth sense, a legacy inherited from their father.

My maternal grandfather died when I was eleven years old. He was Irish and he'd been born with a caul, an inner foetal membrane which is occasionally found covering a baby's head at birth. Traditionally, babies born with a caul are believed to have psychic abilities or *The Sight*, as it is sometimes called.

From an early age I accepted that my grandfather *knew* things.

He could predict events with uncanny accuracy and on occasion a certain sequence of signs would warn him that someone he knew well was going to pass away unexpectedly. Unfortunately the accuracy did not actually extend to the identity of the person. After accidentally overhearing a worried conversation between my grandmother and grandfather one day, I remember sitting at their long kitchen table staring pensively at uncles, aunts and cousins and wondering if it was one of them who was not long for this world.

As well as *The Sight*, my grandfather had piercing blue eyes which seemed to penetrate right into one's very soul.

Often, when one of my cousins or I had done something naughty (which he couldn't possibly have known about), one long look from him was all it took for the culprit to confess.

When I was five, my cousin Mike and his friend Donald invited me to explore an old derelict house which was just down the road from my grandparents' home. It was reputed to be haunted. They offered to lift me through the sash window first, before climbing in themselves. But as my feet touched down on the rotten floorboards, they promptly pulled the window down, jammed it shut with a stick and ran off laughing hysterically. And leaving me frozen in terror.

On their way home they encountered my grandfather. Within minutes he was at the window and lifting it to help me out. As I trotted down the road at his side, I asked him if the house was really haunted. His blue eyes gazed into the distance for a long moment before he replied.

'It's an unhappy house,' he said finally. ' I think something very sad has happened there.'

My cousin Mike told me that it moved a few inches closer to the road every year. Especially when it rained, he said. But I think he may have been lying. I spent many hours standing on the narrow little pavement in the pouring rain watching that house. And I never once saw it move.

When I was in my teens, I became aware that I, too, had inherited my grandfather's sixth sense. Although sometimes it seemed more like five and three-quarters because it refused to be channelled or controlled.

For me, the problem lay in separating premonition from an overactive imagination. I was never quite sure.

I didn't see Carol for a few days and then one morning just before opening time she came into the library in quite a state.

'Never again!' she burst out when she saw me.

'Pardon?'

'Never again will I work alone in this building at night.'

'Why not?' I eyed her speculatively.

'The place is haunted! There was someone watching me all the time. It gave me the creeps!'

'Was your grandfather born with a caul?'

'What?'

'Your grandfather. Was he born with a caul?'

'What's a caul?'

'Never mind. I just wondered.'

'I've told my husband Kevin that he'll have to come with me from now on. He can sit and read in the reading room while I'm working.'

'Sitting in the reading room is not a good idea,' I said slowly. 'Not the reading room and not the passage.'

'Well I don't care what he does, as long as he's here with me.'

Kevin was a brave man. On the first night he spent one and a half hours in the reading room. On the second night, thirty minutes was all it took for him to announce that he was going home. She could come with him or she could stay, he told Carol; it was entirely her decision. She left with him.

Apparently on that second night, it was already dark when they entered the building. While Carol busied herself in the shell room, Kevin settled back in an easy chair in the reading room with a western. He hadn't been there long when he heard something tapping in the passage.

The passage began at the storeroom at the far end of the building and ran between the library area and the shell room, ending in a brick wall just beyond the toilet and bathroom entrance. On the other side of this wall lay the reading room.

'At first the tapping was muffled, but I could hear it through the wall,' Kevin told me. 'As I sat listening, it came closer and closer until it sounded as if it was just on the other side of the wall. Then suddenly it was in the reading room itself. There were three taps, as clear as a bell, and then it stopped. Just like that.'

And that was when he felt that someone was in the room with him.

I listened to his story in bemused silence. What neither he nor Carol knew was that before the alterations to the building, the brick wall had been a doorway into the reading room. When the alterations were in the planning stage, Mr Haig had suggested that the doorway be bricked up. He said that from a security point of view, it would be better if there was only one exit and entrance to the reading room. I had agreed. The reading room housed the reference section and some of the books were very old and quite valuable.

After his experience, Kevin flatly refused to accompany Carol at night and, like me, she took to working over weekends and on Wednesday afternoons.

A few months later one of the elderly library members mentioned in passing that she had known the previous owner of the building. He had lived there for most of his life, she said. When he passed away, the municipality had bought the house from his heirs and converted it into a library.

'Of course, towards the end of his life he was totally blind,' she said. 'But despite this he coped very well. At least once a week I'd join him for afternoon tea and, do you know,' she smiled reminiscently, 'I can still hear the sound of him tapping his way down the passage. With a tray in one hand

and his white stick in the other.'

So could I.

As the provincial library van pulled out of the parking lot, I waved and then turned and walked back into the library. Boxes of new books lay scattered around the floor and, squatting down next to them, I began unpacking.

Every three months or so, staff from the provincial library services based in Port Elizabeth would visit, bringing new stock and taking back any old damaged books I wished to return.

It was like having Christmas four times a year. The boxes were treasure troves of books that still retained the crisp clean smell of the printers and each one was covered in a smooth gleaming plastic cover. My excitement grew as I unpacked, as did the stack of books which I intended to read. That very day. Eventually, I forced myself to select two from the pile and put the rest aside for a 'New Book' display.

Space was always limited and the only display area available was a waist-high bookcase which I had placed in the open lobby between the children's and the adults' section. I stood the books on the three shelves of the bookcase, with the front half of their jacket covers facing forward.

One of the books I placed on the top shelf was *Earthworks* by Lyall Watson, a book about the paranormal. It had a very striking cover. Against a darkish blue background, a foetus lay curled up in a globe resembling the earth. The image was eye-catching and thought-provoking, and I made a mental note to read it soon.

That afternoon was a busy one as members flocked in to

take out the new books. At one stage there was a slight lull and I took advantage of it to use the bathroom. As I hurried past the display I'd set up that morning, I noticed that one of the books had been turned around so that the back half of its jacket cover faced the lobby. I paused briefly to swivel the book. It was *Earthworks* by Lyall Watson.

By closing time I felt drained. Picking up my handbag and car keys, I walked wearily over to the light switches in the alcove. On my way back to the front door, I saw that one of the books on display was facing the wrong way again. When I turned it around, I saw that it was *Earthworks* by Lyall Watson.

Over the next three days, each time I passed the display, my hand would flick out automatically to turn the one book always standing back to front.

At lunchtime on the fourth day I checked the shell room to make sure that all the visitors had left before I locked up. They had, and so I closed the door to the shell room and walked towards the front door. As I drew level with the display I stopped and stared. *Earthworks* was facing the wrong way yet again.

I rolled my eyes in exasperation and reached out to rotate it. Why was it always this book, I wondered? The other books were behaving perfectly. Was it possible that some members of the public found the cover offensive and were turning it deliberately? This seemed unlikely. Shaking my head, I locked up and left.

At ten minutes to three I returned to the library. I unlocked the door and walked over to switch on the lights – and stopped dead in my tracks.

Nestled between four other books, the back cover of *Earthworks* almost seemed to gloat at me.

'This is impossible!' I exclaimed in disbelief. 'The library's been closed. How on earth could this happen?'

I went to my desk and sat there for a few moments, deep in thought. Some form of vibration must be causing the book to swivel. It couldn't be an earth tremor because I would've felt it, especially if it was happening several times a day. Maybe traffic outside in the road was creating vibrations, but then again why would it cause only one of the books to pivot? Why not all of them?

After a while, I rose and went over to the display. I removed the other four books from the top shelf, leaving *Earthworks* standing on its own. Lifting my arm, I banged repeatedly on the shelf with my fist. Despite the thudding blows, the book remained stubbornly in place. It didn't even twitch. Eventually I stopped and stared at it, thoroughly perplexed.

'OK,' I muttered, coming to a sudden decision. 'I've had enough of you.'

I grabbed the book and marched over to the non-fiction section, where I slid it into place amongst the others in its category.

'If you want to be paranormal,' I said severely, ' you can do it on the shelves. And NOT in my display.'

Smash and Grab

A brisk breeze ruffled my hair and sent the inflated chair scudding across the pool. I lolled back in it, gazing up at the sky and watching the clouds change shape. I saw a huge dragon with puffs of smoke streaming from its nostrils suddenly stretch and reform until a castle stood in its place. Complete with turrets and flagpoles.

'Mo.. ommm.'

The castle swirled and shifted and threads of white vapour splayed out, coalescing again within seconds to send a Viking ship sailing across the sky. I could almost hear the mournful call of the long ram's horn.

'MOM!'

'Yes, Nic!'

'Dad says he needs you in the surgery.'

'Did you tell him I'm in the pool?'

'Yes, but he's busy with an emergency and he can't come to you.'

'Tell him I'll be there in a minute.'

'Hurry, he says it's urgent.'

When I entered the surgery, Dave and Johannes were performing an emergency Caesarean on a bulldog. Dave glanced up as I walked in.

'Love, I'm sorry, I know it's your afternoon off,' he said, 'but Ruth has just been here. She says there's a young seal in difficulty in the sea.'

'What sort of difficulty?'

'She thinks it might be sick or injured. It's trying to come out on to the shore but people are standing around where it needs to come out.'

'Why doesn't she ask them to move away?'

'She did, but there's a man fishing opposite the seal and he refuses to budge. Ruth is afraid it might drown.'

'Why are you telling me this?'

'I thought that maybe you could go down and get the fisherman to move and then catch the seal and bring it in.'

'Me?'

'Yes.'

'But Dave, you know I've never handled a seal before. You and Johannes have always done it.'

'I know, but we'll be busy here for at least another hour and then it might be too late. Take a crate with you.'

'Why me, Lord? Why always me?' I muttered as I loaded the crate into the back of the bakkie.

I was scared of seals. Although I'd never handled one, I'd watched Dave, Johannes and a conservation officer trying to tube a seal once. The huge thrashing beast had heaved its body all over the consulting room floor, while simultaneously trying to sink its teeth into various parts of their anatomy. Some of them quite sensitive areas. I had realised then that working with seals is not for the faint-hearted. The splendid ringside view I'd had of two rows of lethally pointed, filthy, foul-smelling fangs had only served to reinforce my fear.

'Let this cup pass from my lips,' was my general attitude when it came to seals.

I remembered Hilary's daughter Jansci telling me about the time she had been bitten on the wrist by one, when she worked at the oceanarium in Port Elizabeth.

'The wound was so deep that it took an hour before it started bleeding,' she'd told me. 'And when it did, the blood just pumped out. *It just pumped out.*'

The words had a certain resonance to them and they had stuck in my mind. As I drove down to the beach I could hear them reverberating in the sound of the engine.

It just pumped out it just pumped out it just . . .

As I parked the bakkie in the parking lot overlooking the beach I could see a group of people standing at the waterline. Amongst them was a short fat man wearing bathing trunks and a red cap. He was holding a fishing rod. As I walked towards them I spotted the seal. It was wallowing clumsily in the first wave and as another wave swept in, it was rolled over and over. There was obviously something wrong.

The group of spectators were very concerned and when I explained the need for them to move away they cooperated immediately. But not the fisherman. He shot me one dismissive look and stood his ground.

'Excuse me,' I said. 'Would you mind moving away so that the seal can come out. I'm going to try and catch it.'

'There's plenty more where it came from,' he sneered.

'That may be so,' I said calmly, 'but this one needs help.'

He ignored me and glowered out to sea.

'Sir, would you like me to call Nature Conservation and have them remove you forcibly?' I asked in dulcet tones, savouring the sudden image of him being dragged across the sand by several burly men in khaki uniforms.

He glared at me malevolently but he began reeling in his line. Once he'd stomped off down the beach, I moved up towards the dunes and squatted down to wait. It didn't take long.

Within minutes the young seal heaved itself out on to the sand. It was about one and a half metres long and extremely emaciated. It collapsed in an exhausted heap just above the waterline with its eyes closed and its breath coming in short gasps.

I stood up and began moving towards it, slowly, one step at a time. When I was two metres away, its eyes flicked open and its head came up. I remained absolutely still as its head swayed from side to side, warning me to keep my distance. But after a while even this activity seemed to tire it, and with a shuddering sigh it dropped its head on to the wet sand once more and lay watching me with dark liquid eyes.

Quickly, before my courage could desert me, I swooped forward and gripped the loose skin behind its head. After one half-hearted attempt at biting me it went limp in my grasp and I lifted it, supporting its belly with my other arm, and hurried across the sand towards the bakkie.

Back at the surgery, Dave was putting in the final stitches. When he was finished, he and Johannes carried the crate from the bakkie into the hospital. He asked me to stay and help them with the tubing.

'OK,' I said, 'I'll anchor its hindquarters while you and Johannes insert the tube.'

I waited until they had hold of its head before I knelt down on the floor and grasped its rear end firmly. Its fur felt thick and soft under my hands and I ran my eyes over its body.

The two broad front flippers were coated in short grey-brown fur which looked like velvet and I noticed that its hindquarters appeared puny in comparison to the powerful

shoulders and front flippers. Below the waist its body seemed to taper off abruptly into two flimsy hind flippers. It was as if God had been momentarily distracted during its creation and had turned back to it murmuring, 'Now where was I? Oh yes . . . two hind flippers.'

On the upper surface of each hind flipper were five pointed flattish toenails. They weren't positioned on the tips of the flippers, but were set an inch or so higher up, and I wondered what purpose they served.

At the other end, Dave and Johannes were battling. While Dave gripped its head, Johannes was trying to slip a loop of crêpe bandage over its lower jaw without getting bitten. Unfortunately each time his fingers got close enough to slip the loop on, the seal would snap at them with vicious intent. Dave's index fingers were also in a vulnerable position, as he exerted pressure on the corners of the seal's mouth, trying to keep the mouth open long enough for Johannes to slip the loop on. I was glad I was at the blunt end.

Eventually Johannes managed to get the loop in place over the lower jaw and another loop over the upper jaw. He pulled the loops apart, holding the mouth open as Dave inserted the tube and ran a litre of Ringer's Lactate solution into the animal's stomach. When the fluid was in, Dave placed his stethoscope against the seal's chest and listened for a few seconds.

'Its lungs don't sound too good,' he said. 'It'll need a course of antibiotics.'

After injecting the antibiotic and giving it a shot of vitamins, he dewormed it. When he was finished with the treatment we carried it over to the large loose cage and placed it inside on a thick blanket.

That evening, as we sat at the kitchen table, I told Dave what the fisherman had said about there being *'Plenty more where it came from.'*

Dave shook his head. ' You should have said, *Sir, you are a ****, and there are plenty more where you come from!*' he snorted.

'I never thought of that,' I grinned, filing the phrase away for future use.

'We'll have to try and get it through to the oceanarium tomorrow.'

'Why can't we just treat it and release it here on the beach when it's recovered?'

'Johannes and I don't have the time to tube a seal three times a day.'

'Won't it take fish?'

'It's unlikely. We've never yet handled a seal that was prepared to take fish from our hands. We've always had to force-feed them, and that's as time-consuming as tubing.'

'Oh.'

'Anyway, the staff at the oceanarium are far more experienced in handling seals than we are. They do it every day.'

'Yes, I suppose so,' I nodded, remembering Jansci's wrist.

Early the next morning I popped in to the hospital to check on the seal. When I opened the cage, it was sitting up looking alert and I stared at it thoughtfully. After a while I closed the cage door and went over to the fridge, where I removed a few defrosted fish and placed them in a bowl.

As I held a fish out to it, it lunged forward and I jerked backwards, dropping the pilchard. The seal peered down at it curiously for a few seconds. Then it leaned forward to sniff at it, as if to assure itself that this was indeed a fish. Suddenly, to my amazement, it picked the fish up in its mouth and began crunching at it. As I watched, the fish was rapidly transformed into an ex-fish. When it resembled nothing more than a mangled wad of flesh and scales, the seal threw its head back and swallowed it.

'That was very clever of you,' I smiled approvingly. 'Can I interest you in another?'

When the third fish had disappeared down its throat, it belched loudly and a wave of putrid breath billowed out at me. Obviously oral hygiene was not high on a seal's list of priorities.

When I went back to the house I found Dave sitting on the pool steps, a mug of coffee in his hand.

'Oh, by the way, we won't have to find someone to take the seal through to the oceanarium,' I called out casually.

He turned to look at me. 'Why? Is it dead?'

'No. It's eating.'

'Eating what?'

'Fish.'

'Who fed it the fish?'

'Me. It took three.'

He stared at me silently, a strange expression on his face.

'Anyway,' I said blandly, 'I must get ready for work now. I'll feed it again at lunchtime.'

I could feel his eyes boring into my back as I walked away.

I sat at my desk, staring pensively at the overdue notice I'd just completed.

A few days after I'd removed the book *Earthworks* from the display and shelved it in the non-fiction section, it'd been taken out by a young man named Brian. No sooner had he taken it out, than I received several enquiries from members who wanted to read the book. Now eight weeks down the line, Brian still had the book, despite my sending him overdue reminders once a week.

One of the people on the waiting list was a professor who was becoming increasingly irascible about my apparent inability to retrieve the book. He had taken to calling in twice a week to find out if it had been returned yet and I was beginning to feel a bit desperate. I explained to him that I was doing my utmost and that I'd sent out six overdue notices and had made several telephone calls, but he wasn't satisfied.

'Surely you could go to his home and demand that he give you the book,' he remarked petulantly.

'I've tried. The house looks deserted. One of the neighbours said that Brian has gone to live with his family in Cape Town.'

'Well, contact him there.'

'Not one of his friends can supply me with an address or contact number. They say his mail is being forwarded to him but they don't know by whom.'

'This is not good enough,' the professor huffed irritably. 'I think I'll have to have a word with Mr Haig.'

'By all means do so,' I replied coldly. 'Maybe he can produce an address from a hat. Or hire a private investigator.'

The professor glared at me and I stared back at him resentfully. Really, I thought, watching him march out the door, his back as stiff as a ramrod, this book was becoming an inconvenient book.

When I walked into the house at lunchtime, our inconvenient dog was sprawled in the middle of the sitting room floor gnawing at a massive bone. The other four dogs were gathered around her, eyeing the bone enviously.

I was staring down at the bone, wondering where she had found it, when the telephone rang.

It was our neighbour Marika, and she sounded distraught. She told me that earlier that morning she had left a side of mutton on the table in her back garden to defrost. Later when she went to check on it, she was just in time to see a large black and tan dog run off with the mutton in its mouth and leap over the fence into our garden.

'I think it was your Dobermann,' she said.

'It was Jade all right,' I said grimly.

Marika explained that the mutton actually belonged to the church and she had been asked to cook it for the church bazaar which was to be held the following day.

'Marika, I'm terribly sorry,' I apologised. 'And of course I'll cover the cost of replacing it.'

When she mentioned the price, I reeled in horror.

'I'm so sorry, Chrystal, but it was a huge roast. More like half a sheep.'

Replacing the receiver, I stormed back into the sitting room. Jade was sucking happily at the bone, strings of saliva dangling from her lips. Before she knew what was happening, I had ripped the bone from her mouth.

'Holy sheep! This cost an absolute fortune,' I seethed, lashing out at her with the bone and missing.

'You miserable thieving dog!'

She scrambled up and lurched towards the door.

'It would've fed us for TWO WHOLE WEEKS!' I called after her.

Sighing heavily, I turned back to the other dogs.

'Here, Beau,' I said, holding out the bone to her. 'You might as well have what's left.'

Beau gazed at it with distaste.

'I'm not putting my mouth on THAT,' she shrivelled her lips fastidiously. *'It's covered in Jade's bodily fluids.'*

'It's only a bit of spit.'

' "Saliva" is classified as a bodily fluid,' she observed stubbornly. *'Consult any medical dictionary or handbook.'*

'*I'll have it*,' Arrow offered, a sanctimonious expression upon her face.

'OK then,' I said, with a pointed look at Beau. 'I'll just rinse it off for you, shall I?'

Sealed with a Fish

'RUN FOR YOUR LIFE,' I shrieked. 'HERE COMES SMASH!'

In mid-stride, Jade, Cubby, Arrow and Flenny turned tail and hurtled up the steps on to the patio, with me and Beau hot on their heels. As I cleared the top step, I flung the fish I'd been clutching in my hand. It landed in the middle of the deep end of the pool with a splash and Smash streaked past us and into the water.

The young seal was a male and we had named him 'Smash' because of what he did to fish prior to swallowing them. Initially Dave had kept Smash in hospital for a few days while he was receiving the daily antibiotic injections, but we knew that this arrangement could only be temporary. By the end of a day, the stench from his cage was quite overwhelming and several clients had shown a tendency to faint. The manpower required to restrain him made it impractical to clean the cage more than once a day. Apart from this consideration, Smash needed to swim and build up condition before we could release him. We estimated that this would take approximately three weeks.

Shortly after we moved in to The Greenhouse, Dave had commissioned a handyman to erect a permanent enclosure for penguins in our garden. We decided to position it in a clearing near to the boundary wall between ourselves and one of our next door neighbours.

The neighbours were fascinated by the penguins and would hang over the wall watching them. When Smash was ready to be moved from the hospital, Dave went out and bought a few metres of rigid, free-standing wire. He and Johannes nailed one end of this wire to one of the perimeter poles of the penguin enclosure. Forming a semicircular run, they tied the other end to a second pole, in order to be able to open and close it when necessary. The free-standing wire was about one metre high and we thought that it was more than adequate to confine one young seal. We were wrong.

By the time Smash was transferred to the garden, he was consuming vast quantities of fish. He never seemed to have his fill and it was a simple matter to get him up to the pool for a swim and then back again into the run. All you needed was fish.

I'd approach the run, waggling a fish enticingly in one hand. With my other hand, I'd undo the ties attaching the wire to the pole and then, flinging open the wire, I'd run for the steps. At first the dogs viewed these activities as a thrilling new game and they joined in enthusiastically. But after a few narrow shaves they realised that this was a serious business. He who hesitated ran the risk of being mistaken for a fish. And by now, we all knew what Smash did to his fish. And another thing we all knew was that one must never look back.

'Don't look back!' I'd yell to the dogs. 'Whatever you do, don't look back!'

On the first day I made the mistake of looking back and I nearly came a cropper. Unnerved by Smash's close proximity to my heels, I tripped and almost fell. It was touch and go, really.

One Saturday morning, as I opened the enclosure and turned to run, I heard a voice say, 'Hello Chrystal.' To my dismay I spotted Dodo and Bill standing at the top of the steps.

'RUN!' I shouted urgently as I took off. 'HERE COMES SMASH!'

I must hand it to them, they showed an amazing turn of speed for their age. They were both in their eighties but they covered the distance between the steps and the sliding doors in seconds. By the time Smash flashed past me and into the pool, they were already in the sitting room. With the sliding doors firmly shut.

Early the next morning I emerged from the surgery with a bucket of fish in my hand, unaware that Dave had entered the pool and was scrubbing at the walls with a wire brush. As the dogs and I reached the top step I saw him and screamed, 'Dave, GET OUT!'

There was a second of stunned silence and then Dave's hand shot out and seized the barbecue grid which happened to be lying on the bricks next to the edge of the pool. He thrust the grid over his groin. It was in the nick of time because a second after he did so, Smash's snout brushed up against the grid.

By the time Dave had edged out of the pool, I was leaning against the outer sitting room wall, giggling weakly.

'Chrystal,' he said heavily, 'this is no laughing matter. It could've been nasty.'

'I know that,' I spluttered. 'I'm giggling because I got such a fright.'

'In future I think you should check the pool before letting Smash out.'

'I will, I will, I'm sorry,' I said, dissolving once more into giggles.

Looking bleak, Dave stalked off into the bedroom, still carrying the barbecue grid.

Actually, I was beginning to have my suspicions about Smash's aggression. To me, there seemed to be an element of 'all bark and no bite' about his actions.

But I wasn't certain.

On a Wednesday, exactly three weeks to the day that I'd brought him in, we decided to release Smash. I worked half-days on Wednesdays and Dave suggested that we do the release when I arrived home at lunchtime.

Ushered in by a fish, Smash entered the wooden cage happily and we loaded it into the back of the bakkie and drove the hundred or so metres to the beach. We placed the cage on the dry sand just above the high-water mark and when we opened the door, Smash emerged cautiously. For a few moments he sat absolutely still, his head swinging from side to side as he surveyed his surroundings intently. And then he took off.

He crossed the short stretch of sand at a gallop and as the first wave surged in his body seemed to melt into it. He disappeared from sight below the frothing water and we waited for him to surface. Suddenly his head bobbed up in the surf beyond the fourth wave and I marvelled at the speed at which he could travel through water. No one was more aware than I that he was not exactly a tortoise on land either. But this was different.

Sea and seal seemed to embrace each other, to meld together. His ponderous, clumsy movements on land were transformed into mercurial movements of fluid grace, as if the waves were partnering him in a sweeping waltz. It struck me forcibly that his body had been designed for the sea. This was his element. It was where he belonged and, watching him, I wished that I could experience such exquisite harmony of movement with the waves.

Smash seemed in no hurry to move off further into the bay and eventually Dave and I carried the cage back to the bakkie and drove home.

Late that afternoon, taking Beau and Arrow with me, I walked down to the beach and stood at the top of the steps, gazing out to sea. Beyond the last breaker I could see something dark gliding slowly through the water, dragging ripples in its wake. It was Smash. As I watched, one of his flippers came up and waved lazily in the air, as he rolled on to his side. He seemed perfectly at ease, but I wondered why he was not on his way home to the islands.

It was so different when penguins were released. After a brief pause to synchronise their compasses, they would move off in a tight pack, as if drawn by a powerful magnetic force. Penguins came into this world with built-in homing devices, but I wasn't quite sure how it worked with seals.

Thursday morning was exceptionally quiet at the library and I took the opportunity to catch up on a backlog of administrative work. Just before lunchtime, Dave phoned me to say that one of his clients had reported seeing a seal on the beach early that morning. The seal had been on its way to the steps, but when it saw the client it had turned back and re-entered the water.

'Dave, I'm closing up here now,' I told him. 'I need to deliver some books to one of our elderly members. On the way home I'll stop off at the beach and check for Smash.'

I replaced the receiver and walked over to shut the windows in the reading room. As I stepped into the room, I came to an abrupt halt.

One third of the reading room was taken up by a long wooden table, which was used mostly by children working on school projects. In the centre of its gleaming brown surface lay a single book. *Earthworks*, by Lyall Watson.

Gooseflesh whistled down my arms and legs, as I stared at the book in disbelief. For a few seconds my mind went absolutely blank and then it whirred into action, seeking some rational explanation.

Was Brian back in town? Had he deliberately left the book in the reading room, to avoid paying the overdue fine? But Brian hadn't been in the library that morning. I would've seen him if he had. Maybe a friend of his then? It had been unusually quiet that morning. Only five people had used the library and not one of them had any connection with Brian, as far as I knew. Maybe Brian had lost the book and someone else had found it and returned it. But why would they leave it in the reading room? Why not hand it in at the counter? I hadn't seen anyone using the reading room that morning. Ah, I thought, perhaps someone had tossed it through one of the windows? My eyes drifted to the windows. The gaps in the burglar proofing were far too narrow to allow for the passage of a hard-covered book.

'You're not a book, you're a phenomenon,' I muttered, picking it up and carrying it back to the counter. 'And I wish you would just go away now.' Anyway, at least the professor would be pleased.

When I stopped off at the beach, there was no sign of Smash.

'Hopefully he's on his way back to the islands,' I said to Dave.

At nine o'clock that night, there was a loud knock on the front door. Dave was busy in the surgery and I opened it to find a young man on the doorstep.

'I'm sorry to trouble you at this time of night,' he apologised, 'but a seal has just crossed the main road at the filling station on the corner. And we don't know what to do with it.'

When I arrived at the scene, a group of people were standing around an upturned milk crate which was lying on the pavement. The crate seemed far too small to contain a seal I thought, eyeing it doubtfully.

'Are you sure it's a seal?' I asked the young man.

He assured me that it was. I asked the people to move back and, squatting down, I lifted the crate.

The seal was lying flat on the concrete, eyes shut, front flippers pressed tightly against its sides. It was a very compressed seal.

'Smash?' I murmured.

At the sound of my voice, his eyes flicked open and his head jerked up, an expression of pure relief on his face.

'*Thank God it's YOU!*' his face seemed to say.

Reaching out, I stroked him gently and he made no attempt to bite me. He was quite a weight now and the young man offered to drive us back to the house. As I perched on the seat next to him, cradling Smash in my arms, he told me that he had been parked at one of the petrol pumps when a little boy in the vehicle behind his had cried out, 'MOM... LOOK! There's a seal crossing the road!'

'Jason, seals don't cross roads,' the mother had sighed irritably. 'It must be a dog. And I've warned you before about telling fibs.'

'But Mom...'

'Another word and you'll get a hiding.'

Smash seemed relieved to be back in his run and after a bedtime snack of twelve pilchards, he settled down contentedly for the night.

But early the next morning when I went to check I sensed a restlessness in him. He was moving from one side of the run to the other, nudging at the wire, as if seeking an escape route.

'It was your decision to come back,' I told him.

On the Saturday morning I went to the surgery to prepare fish for him. As I bustled around the small kitchen, separating fish into a large bowl, I happened to glance out through the small back window.

Smash was sitting at the barred metal gate which divided the back garden from the surgery area. How on earth had he managed to get out of the run, I wondered?

He hadn't spotted me yet and was bobbing up and down, craning his neck and trying to peer in through the back door of the surgery. Moving quietly, I stuck my head around the door and said, 'Good morning, are you hungry?'

His reaction was instantaneous. With one despairing look, his eyes seemed to roll back in his head as he slumped down on to the ground and lay there unmoving. Thoroughly alarmed, I rushed out. His catatonic body was wedged against the gate, preventing me from opening it. He did not appear to be breathing and I reached through the bars and shook him vigorously.

'Smash, wake up, WAKE UP!' I cried, beginning to panic. There was an infinitesimal movement in his chest area and a faint whisper of breath sifted through his lips. As he lay there comatose, a single tear formed at the corner of one eye. It trailed down his cheek, through his whiskers and dripped on to the ground.

I sprang up and raced back into the surgery.

'DAVE, DAVE, there's something the matter with Smash!'

'Doctor is out on a call,' Johannes shouted from the hospital.

'Johannes, try and get hold of him. Tell him it's urgent. Smash is dying!'

As I stood in the middle of the kitchen trying to decide what to do, I glanced out through the window again.

Smash was sitting up at the gate, eyes bright and alert as he peered hopefully at the open back door.

'Umm, Johannes?' I said slowly.

'Yes?'

'Er, don't bother the doctor now. I think Smash will be fine.'

When I stepped through the door carrying the bowl of fish, Smash bounced up and down gleefully.

'You'll have to move away from the gate, so that I can open it,' I informed him sternly. His face beamed up at me.

'And if you EVER try and pull a stunt like that again,' I hissed, 'I'll ship you straight to Hollywood.' I wondered fleetingly whether he and Philby did not perhaps share some distant genetic connection. Some imprint of the stars.

Dave looked cynical when I described the incident to him.

'Dave, I'm not exaggerating,' I insisted. 'It was a performance worthy of an Oscar.'

'Hmmmm. Anyway, Johannes and I will have to secure the base of the run with tent pegs. We can't have him roaming the garden at will. It's far too dangerous.'

Dodo and Bill had invited us to supper that evening and when we returned home it was to find Smash frolicking energetically in the pool. Dave and I stared at him through the glass of the closed sliding doors.

'How did he manage to get out?'

'I don't know. I'll have to check the tent pegs.'

The tent pegs were all still firmly embedded in the ground. We were absolutely mystified.

'He must have come over the top.'

'Yes, but how? It's not as if he has hind legs and feet to assist him in climbing.'

From what I had observed, Smash's flimsy hind flippers

only appeared to function effectively in conjunction with his powerful front flippers, as if they were merely an aid. The only activity I'd seen them perform independently, was scratching. He would collapse the top part of the flippers, leaving the flat toenails exposed and proceed to scratch meticulously behind his ears and head, almost as if he was scratching himself with his knuckles. These hind flippers of his were not an item of equipment a mountaineer would have on his list of priorities. We weren't talking hobnailed boots here.

We managed to get him back into his run and that night I dreamt of flying seals.

The next morning I was busy making our bed when Nic ran into the bedroom, dripping wet, his face as white as a sheet.

'MOM . . . MOM, Smash was in the pool with me!'

I swung round to gaze at the pool. The surface was smooth, not a ripple in sight.

'Nic, it must be your imagination. Look, there's nothing there.'

'Mom, he's in there, I swear!'

I walked over to the edge of the pool and stared into its depths. As I looked, a trail of delicate bubbles trippled up from the bottom. And suddenly Smash was there. His body sleeked through the air and down again, like a flash of liquid lightning.

Nic told me he'd been snorkelling underwater, when something dark had wafted down past him.

'I thought it was a jersey.'

'What would a jersey be doing in the pool?'

'I thought maybe you'd thrown it in.'

'But why would I throw a jersey into the pool?'

'Mom, sometimes you do strange things.'

And then the jersey had started swimming.

When I went to tell Dave what had happened, he said that Smash would have to go to the oceanarium after all. It was just too risky to have a seal loose in the garden, especially for Nic and the animals.

He telephoned the oceanarium immediately, and as luck would have it, they informed him that Linda, the curator of the oceanarium, was spending the weekend in Dolphin Bay. Dave contacted her and she offered to collect Smash late that afternoon. She said they had two other young seals which they were planning to transport back to the islands in the near future. Smash would get a lift right to his doorstep.

Later that morning, the mystery of how he was managing to get out of the run was solved.

I was busy in the bedroom again when a movement in the garden attracted my attention. I stood at the French windows, partially concealed by the curtains and saw Smash slither up against the wire, until his body was in an upright position. As I watched, he hooked his two front flippers over the wire. Then, heaving with his front flippers and using his hind flippers as a springboard, he sailed over the wire and landed on the grass.

My dream about flying seals had not been too far off the mark.

Linda arrived that afternoon to collect him and I felt a bit weepy as I helped load his cage into her jeep. But I consoled myself with the knowledge that we were doing the right thing for Smash. Now he would be returned to his home ground without having to run the gauntlet of sharks and armed crewmen on fishing boats, who resented having to compete for fish.

All in all, Smash spent just less than four weeks with us. But in those few weeks I learnt so much about seals. My perception of seals had changed completely and I had a much deeper understanding of how their minds worked. And their teeth.

A few days later, the staff at the oceanarium sent us a note. '*Smash is a real cannibal!*' it said.

Two weeks passed before they phoned to tell us that he had been successfully returned to the islands. Apparently, as the boat neared the rocky shore, they'd opened the three wire cages. Smash had taken one look at the familiar shoreline and shot out of his cage and dived overboard. The last they saw of him was a small brown snout swimming determinedly for home.

The other two seals were not quite as enthusiastic. They had to be pushed overboard.

One month after the mysterious return of *Earthworks*, I received a recall notice from the provincial library in Port Elizabeth. The book was required for another library.

I went through the issue drawers. The issue card wasn't there. The book must be on the shelves then, I thought. It wasn't. I searched through the pile of books awaiting repair, but it wasn't there either.

I telephoned the provincial library to explain that the book seemed to have disappeared off the face of the earth. They thanked me for getting back to them so promptly and asked if I'd like another copy when one was available.

I said I didn't think it was necessary.

Dogging My Footsteps

'There's a black eagle in the hospital.'
'Oh, is it sick?'
'No, it's injured.'

Dave told me it had been caught in a gin trap. I hated them, they were such cruel devices. Once the steel jaws slammed shut there was no escape. Leopards had been known to gnaw off a limb when trapped, only to succumb to shock and loss of blood. The traps were often set and left unmonitored for weeks, condemning any victim to a lingering death of fear, excruciating pain and starvation.

I had never seen a black eagle in the flesh and I hurried to the hospital to have a look. Bending down before its cage, I lifted the loose cover hanging over the wire door and peered in.

The eagle was crouched on a thick log to the rear of the cage. The powerful three-inch talons on its right foot were gripping the wood, but I noticed that the talons on the left foot were curled inwards. The left leg was encased in a bandage and was propped up awkwardly on the log.

Dave said the eagle had been caught in the trap over a month before. The trap had shattered the leg, breaking the bone, and the conservation officers who found it had taken it to the nearest vet. He'd applied a Robert-Jones bandage but now, one month later, there was a non-union. The bone had not knitted.

The vet in question ran a large-animal practice in a farming area about a hundred kilometres from Dolphin Bay and he'd approached Dave for help. The eagle's leg needed to be pinned, he said, and his equipment and instruments were geared for larger species.

The eagle, a young male, was fairly thin and debilitated. When Dave examined him, it was obvious that the trauma of the injury, and being held in a cage for a month, had taken its toll. Dave decided to try to boost the bird's general condition before attempting the operation.

He and Johannes spent two days erecting a wooden platform on poles in the walled fountain area off our en suite bathroom. The area was open to the sky and boasted several young trees and a three-tiered fountain standing in a round tiled pond. Thick ivy decked the walls and on the ground flat round stones rested on a surface of moss and peace-in-the-home. It was a peaceful green place, away from human and animal traffic and Dave felt that the eagle would be less stressed in such surroundings.

When the platform was in place, Dave transferred the eagle from the hospital cage. He attached one end of a long jess to the bird's good leg and the other end to one of the poles, enabling him to move freely between the ground and the platform.

The eagle had been in the fountain area for two weeks when Dave approached me one morning as I was about to leave for work.

'Will you feed the eagle at lunchtime?' he asked.

'Why?'

'Johannes and I will be out for most of the day on farm

calls.'

'Why don't you just leave the meat in a bowl and he can help himself?'

'He's still not taking from a bowl. He'll only eat if we hold the meat in our fingers.'

I stared at Dave warily.

'I'm trying to feed him as often as possible, to build him up.'

'Oh.'

To be honest, I was reluctant to become involved with the eagle. He was a truly magnificent bird with his glossy coal-black feathers and his regal looks, but I found the size of his beak and talons a bit off-putting.

'He's not going to bite my fingers, is he?'

'No, he doesn't bite.'

'That's what you said about the barn owl chicks.'

Dave sighed. 'Chrystal, all I can tell you is that he's never attempted to bite me.'

'You said that about the barn owl chicks too.'

'Look, he's not going to bite you. But stay well away from his talons.'

It was a hectic morning at the library and by lunchtime the eagle had slipped from my mind. When I staggered into the house and collapsed into a chair, I found a note propped up on the kitchen table.

Don't forget the eagle.

'Oh damn,' I muttered. 'All this and heaven too.'

In the fridge I found a bowl containing bits of a dead hare which someone had found next to the highway. I grabbed the bowl thinking that I might as well get it over with.

I hurried through to the bathroom, but as I opened the French windows and stepped into the fountain area, I stopped and stared in horror at the scene before me. The eagle was not perched on top of the platform. Nor was he sitting on the ground.

He was hanging upside-down above the pond, the jess around his leg caught on the upper tier of the fountain.

'OH NOOO! What am I going to do nowww,' I groaned.

When I took a closer look at the fountain, I discovered that the jess was actually wound around the top section, as if he'd done several circuits before being suspended.

I stared at the eagle, trying to decide what to do. His wings were fully extended and beating wildly in panic. I could see that any attempt to grip his legs and circle the fountain without securing his wings would cause considerable damage as they would thrash into branches and the fountain itself.

If I gripped his wings with my hands, his talons would be free to wreak havoc in my face and throat area. Cutting the jess would mean that he could fly away, injured leg and all. I couldn't leave him hanging while I went to summon help because he was already hyperventilating from stress, his beak open, his breath coming in panting gasps.

Somehow, I needed to secure both his wings and talons simultaneously.

And then it came to me.

I took a deep breath and stepped into the pond, shoes and all, with my arms outstretched. Clasping his wings, I folded them gently into his body. Then, before he could extend them again, I quickly doubled over. With my face resting against the back of his head, I slid my arms over his shoulders and up to grip his legs. Still bent over double, with my shoulders curved over his wings, I stumbled around the fountain. With his talons resting against my side.

After two circuits, I felt the jess fall free and I straightened slowly and lifted him into an upright position. As I released my grip on his legs, he landed on the ground in a flurry of wings and feathers. He sat there with his chest heaving as he gasped for breath, but after a few minutes his breathing eased.

I stood absolutely still, gazing down into his deep brown eyes and suddenly, the air seemed to quicken as if a current of communication had opened up between us. A thought current.

I felt a heightened sense of consciousness as thoughts thrummed back and forth. And with them came an overwhelming perception of great dignity, combined with an innate kindness.

What kind of bird are you? I wondered silently. That will allow your talons to rest against a human body without clawing that body?

I am an eagle, the thought flew back to me.

Eventually I stirred and, retrieving the bowl of meat, I sat down on the low wall of the pond, facing him. I selected a piece and held it out to him and his focus shifted from me to the meat. Stooping forward slightly, he took the meat gently in his beak and throwing his head back, he swallowed it in one gulp.

We sat together in companionable silence and finally, when the bowl was empty, I rose and walked back into the house.

Two weeks later, Dave performed the pinning. He was assisted by Julia, a vet from Port Elizabeth who had considerable experience of working with raptors. When Dave opened the wound to reach the shattered bone, he found bits of feather, grass and even twig, embedded in the bone. He was amazed that this hadn't resulted in severe infection.

The operation proceeded smoothly and a few hours later, the eagle regained consciousness. He seemed fine and that night he took a few pieces of meat from my fingers.

But on the third day after the operation his condition began deteriorating.

Early that morning, I nipped into the hospital to feed him before I set off for work. When I held the meat out to him he turned his head away and I squatted on the floor before his cage, gazing at him anxiously. I noticed that his eyes seemed dull, almost glazed, and he was crouched lower on the log, as if he was weak.

'Dave, there's something wrong with the eagle.'

'What?'

'He won't eat.'

'Maybe he's not hungry. In the wild he wouldn't be getting regular meals.'

'I think it's more than that.'

That afternoon when I came home from the library, Dave gave me the bad news. Gangrene had set in.

'His temperature is spiking and I've had to change the antibiotic.' Dave said we'd just have to wait and see whether the rampaging infection would respond to the new antibiotic.

The next day he was even weaker. No longer able to grip the log, he huddled listlessly in a corner of the cage. Dave added a second antibiotic to the treatment regime and we watched closely for any sign of an improvement. But there was nothing. It was as if he had lost the will to live.

Dave could not understand why gangrene should set in after the debris of grass and feathers had been removed from the site of the injury. He said it would have been perfectly understandable had this developed before.

The black eagle died on the sixth day after the operation.

It was a bitter blow.

With hindsight, Dave concluded that the trauma of being

trapped combined with the trauma of the operation, had proved to be one trauma too many. It would have been better if the pinning had been performed at the time of the injury.

When the initial heartache eased, I tried to put his death into perspective. We had been worried that even after the pinning, he might not regain the full use of his left leg. If this had been the case, he wouldn't have been able to survive successfully in the wild and would've had to spend the rest of his days in captivity.

He wouldn't have wanted this. Before the operation, I had noticed as I sat with him that his eyes would seek out the sky, as if there was a deep longing in him. Some people call eagles *Children of the Clouds*.

In the end I accepted that the grief I was feeling was for my loss, not his. In a way, death had released his spirit into the sky he had yearned for. Sometimes, in the weeks and months that followed, I almost thought I could see him up there.

Late one afternoon, as I was walking along the beach, I spotted a black speck spiralling on thermals high in the heavens above me. And I wrote a poem to the black eagle in my head.

> *Wind spirit soar the clouds*
> *Wild skysong of the soul*
> *Cumulus sea of solitary peace*
> *Free the earthmind*

As I parked the Beetle in the road opposite our front door, Johannes ran out from the surgery to call me. He said Dave wanted to show me something. When I walked into the waiting room, I could hear the murmur of voices in the consulting room and I hesitated, reluctant to disturb him while he was consulting.

'Doctor is in there,' Johannes gestured.

'I know, but he has someone with him.'

'He wants you to go in.'

'Oh, OK.'

One of our regular clients, Cindy Evans, was standing against the consulting table, holding something in her arms. Dave glanced up as I entered and smiled. 'Look who's here,' he said, nodding towards Cindy.

I looked at Cindy and then my eyes slid down to the animal in her arms. It was a cat.

It was Silverkitty.

'SILVERKITTY!' I cried. I dropped my handbag and rushed over to take him.

'Is it really you?' I asked and he gazed up at me with a pleased smirk. I couldn't believe it was him. After all this time. It had been more than three and a half years since he disappeared. As I hugged him to me, he began purring and tears welled up in my eyes and streamed down my cheeks.

Suddenly I was transported back to the front garden at the old sea-house.

'Why don't you just shut up and fly, mate,' Philby was yelling at a seagull clattering overhead. *'While you still can.'*

Just beyond him, Splittie was delivering a lecture, to no one in particular, on *Overfishing – and the effects thereof.*

Nuggie was crouched on the old wooden table, contemplating the sea and quoting Shakespeare.

'So long as men can breathe, or eyes can see,' he was declaiming dreamily, *'So long lives this, and this gives life to thee.'*

And in the midst of them all, Fluffy lifted her head and

asked vaguely, *'Is it that time already?'*

Then, in a flash, they were gone again and I heard Cindy telling Dave that Silverkitty, now named Stranger, had been living with them for almost a year. She and her husband and their two children were renting a house on the sea front and one day Stranger had strolled out of the dunes and moved in with them.

'Do you know, Dave,' Cindy was saying, 'hearing his history, I'm a bit worried. We're moving to a new house next month, and it's quite a distance from the sea. I wonder if he'll settle?'

I looked at Silverkitty who returned my gaze with an inscrutable expression on his face. I wondered too.

Two months later, Cindy phoned Dave to report that Stranger was missing. She'd fetched him back from their previous house several times. But each time he'd only remain for a day or two, before slipping off again. And now he was nowhere to be found.

When Dave told me this, I shook my head. I had a strong suspicion that, even as we spoke, Silverkitty was sitting down to a fish supper with his new family. Somewhere overlooking the sea.

'Would you pass the tartare sauce, please,' he was asking politely.

Early the next morning, when I awoke, the sound of the sea was loud in the bedroom and I flung off the duvet and responded to its call.

It was still quite dark, dawn a weak, luminous promise on the horizon, when the dogs and I strolled down the road. Beau slotted in behind me, while Cubby, Flenny and Arrow trotted ahead and Jade bucked against her lead at my side.

As we drew level with the house on the corner, Beau veered off and went over to a patch of bright green grass next to the house. She threw herself down and began rolling madly in the thick damp grass, jack-knifing her body and swivelling from side to side in obvious delight. I paused to watch her and remembered Whippy doing the very same thing on the very same patch of grass.

When Beau noticed me watching, she sprang up, embarrassed to be caught in such a silly act. I laughed at her.

'You're allowed to be silly sometimes,' I said and her eyes laughed back at me.

A thick mist had built up over the sea, and as we descended the wooden steps it rolled up on to the beach, quietly, inexorably, enveloping me and the dogs in its clammy silence. Gusts of dense vapour billowed past us cloaking the houses and bush-covered dunes in a white shroud. Visibility was reduced to a couple of metres and when we reached the water's edge, the sea lay before us, a heaving disembodied shadow of its former self, its thundering voice subdued to a hushed roar.

A seagull called close by and before I could react, Jade jerked the lead from my hand and hurtled off into the mist. We heard her hysterical barks fade into the distance.

The beach took on an ethereal quality, an otherworldliness and I was overcome by a sense of timelessness.

As we walked, my feet and the dogs' paws left crisp, clear imprints in the moist sand. I thought about Silverkitty and his affinity for the sea and the beach. It was almost as if he was joined to them by an invisible umbilical chord. And I could relate to that.

My thoughts drifted to Whippy and Mandy and the countless times we'd walked or jogged this very same stretch

of beach together. Sometimes I observed elements of both of them in Beau. Whippy's soppiness and Mandy's cutting edge. The marshmallow paw in the iron glove.

A small wave scurried in and drew back again, leaving tiny translucent shells trapped in our footprints and I remembered Nuggie's first encounter with a wave. I thought about him, and Philby. And Splittie. And Fluffy. I could still feel their presence so strongly. As if, like Jade, they had vanished into the mist and were waiting somewhere up ahead for me to join them. And one day I would. But not just yet.

Suddenly, without warning, a large black shape barrelled into view and slammed right into me, knocking the breath from my body. For a few seconds I was airborne, before I landed heavily on the sand.

It was Jade. As I tried to catch my breath, Beau rushed at her. She struck like a cobra, sinking her teeth into Jade's rump. Agonised yelps rent the air.

'You clumsy clot!' Beau snarled furiously. *'Next time watch where you're going!'*

I lay sprawled on the sand, watching Beau. With her lean, brown-flecked body, her rigid pointed ears and smouldering topaz eyes, she looked every inch the wolf.

As I rose stiffly to my feet, it occurred to me that there was a second wolf I was running with now.

And I wondered if I would be able to maintain the pace.